"This book is a gem. Crosby and Lippert take this complex and...sometimes confusing experience...of...living with attention deficit/hyperactivity disorder (ADHD), and make it imminently understandable. And then they provide a plethora of interesting and doable ideas, as well as...practical...strategies for you...to live the life you want. NOW."

—**Susan Marie, PMHNP, PhD**, associate professor at Oregon Health and Science University, and senior medical director for Behavioral Health in Primary Care, Central City Concern

"*Transforming ADHD* strikes that right balance of information that comes both from the 'head and the heart.' Crosby and Lippert provide practical strategies to help adults function better with ADHD that not only are solidly based in the research literature, but also come from a wealth of both clinical and personal experience.... ADHD affects adults in so many different ways.... The authors understand the impact ADHD has on individuals' lives, and the book provides tips that adults can apply in their work and family life along with lots of supportive advice.... They really get what it's like to live with ADHD."

—**Bradley Steinfeld, PhD**, assistant director at Group Health Cooperative Behavioral Health Services

"*Transforming ADHD* is a clearly written and easy-to-use guide for overcoming ADHD and literally rewiring your attention! If this sounds complicated, it's not—because authors Crosby and Lippert weave together engaging, real-life stories, research, brain science, and relationship patterns to re-envision ADHD.... Best of all, they offer a set of practical, daily skills and mindful awareness tools for overcoming procrastination and increasing your effectiveness....Whether you're an adult diagnosed with ADHD, or a mental health clinician working in the ADHD field, *Transforming ADHD* is an essential key to unlocking the ADHD puzzle. A...must-have book!"

> —**Donald Altman, MA, LPC**, author of the best-selling *The Mindfulness Toolbox, Clearing Emotional Clutter,* and *One-Minute Mindfulness*

"As someone who has had the privilege of having a front row seat to witness Greg Crosby lead workshops for attorneys with ADHD, I anticipated that this book that he partnered with Tonya Lippert to produce would be a solid, research-based resource. It has exceeded my positive expectations. It is written in a clear and efficient style.... Their guiding metaphor of flashing lights and guiding lights provided a great focus or lens for the research-based strategies and tools they offer.... I appreciated how they were able to relate and reinforce material and tools which they introduced at the start of the book with the material and tools that they followed with.... I believe that the population which I work with, attorneys, will find this book to be a helpful and easy-to-digest resource."

> —**Mike Long**, attorney counselor, Oregon Attorney Assistance Program

TRANSFORMING

ADHD

SIMPLE, EFFECTIVE ATTENTION & ACTION REGULATION SKILLS TO HELP YOU FOCUS & SUCCEED

GREG CROSBY, MA, LPC
TONYA K. LIPPERT, PhD

New Harbinger Publications, Inc.

The Relationship Structures (ECR-RS) Questionnaire by R. Chris Fraley, copyright © 2006 by R. Chris Fraley. Reprinted by permission of the author.

Distributed in Canada by Raincoast Books

Copyright © 2016 by Greg Crosby and Tonya K. Lippert
New Harbinger Publications, Inc.
5674 Shattuck Avenue
Oakland, CA 94609
www.newharbinger.com

Cover design by Amy Shoup

Acquired by Melissa Kirk

Edited by Melanie Bell

All Rights Reserved

FSC
www.fsc.org
MIX
Paper from
responsible sources
FSC® C011935

Library of Congress Cataloging-in-Publication Data on file

18   17   16

10   9   8   7   6   5   4   3   2   1   First Printing

We dedicate this book to all whose wandering attention and action led them to us. We hope they will be proud of what we've learned from them.

"Everyone knows what attention is. It is the taking possession by the mind, in clear and vivid form, of one out of what seem several simultaneously possible objects or trains of thought. Focalization, concentration, of consciousness are of its essence."

—William James, *The Principles of Psychology*

Contents

Introduction

Leena earns enough money that she could save up for the things she wants to do, such as travel, but instead she often struggles to pay the bills. Her car is her biggest expense. Traffic and parking tickets eat at her potential savings at a rate of about a thousand dollars a month.

George has some struggles, too. He just started a new job a few months ago and, at first, loved it. Now he's anxious at work. He's making mistakes that would cost his company big time except that his boss keeps catching them. He often leaves work late both trying to fix mistakes and volunteering to do unpaid things at work, such as hosting events and helping colleagues with their projects.

Leena and George have both been diagnosed with ADHD. The specific ways that their ADHD shows up look different but the underlying patterns of behavior are the same: forgetfulness, careless mistakes, disorganization, distractibility, staying "on the go," and restlessness. And they are exhibited to a degree that crosses the line from ordinary to extreme, with heavy consequences.

You may have been diagnosed with ADHD for the same reasons as Leena or George or because you procrastinate doing things that require mental effort over a long time period, have trouble following through, interrupt, talk excessively, or find it hard to wait. And you've probably suffered unwanted consequences, too.

You've also probably tried some adjustments, knowing what comes easy for you and what comes hard. Perhaps you've found jobs with relatively flexible schedules that require less routine and reward novelty seeking. You may have sought out relationships where your differences work.

But you want more. It's likely you're reading this book to know how to use the latest and greatest understanding of ADHD to transform your life. You've come to the right place.

An Overview of ADHD

Imagine, for a moment, old-fashioned scales…the kind that tip down on one side and up on the other when the sides are imbalanced. The prevailing story of ADHD has spotlighted one side of the scales: the side of your attention and action that boredom, disinterest, and tedium weigh down. Its counterweight, the side that excitement, interest, and novelty elevate, has remained a side note. In fact, you may hardly hear about this side. But to understand ADHD and the skills you can practice to get what you really want, you need to know it. You need to see both sides of ADHD—underfocus *and* overfocus—and the factors that move each side of the scale.

Underfocus

When you face tasks of little interest to you, particularly future-oriented ones, the defining underfocus and distractibility of ADHD often rear their head. You likely struggle with everyday tasks such as listening; remembering instructions, dates, and appointments; checking the mail; and paying bills. Add impulsiveness and little patience for frustration, and your happiness, relationships, and accomplishments can suffer. As you try to keep up with everyday tasks, you may feel as if you are running all the time without covering much distance. And yet if you ask, "Where *is* my attention?" you can find it. You just need to know where to look.

Overfocus

To find your attention, look at what things interest you the most. What are you doing when no one tells you what to do? The overfocus side of ADHD often shows up for such things as playing sports, searching online for something interesting to you, starting a spontaneous creative project (such as creating a funny video to post), socializing with friends and family, pursuing a novel idea or action, playing video games, or watching TV. It's where your attention goes when it's free.

The fact that the other side of ADHD, underfocus, has defined the diagnosis has created problems. First, skills practice likely has targeted doing more of what ordinary people do to stay organized, on task, and on time, and ignored how to use your mind's particular inclinations to your advantage. Second, because you can focus on things highly interesting and exciting to you, others have likely had a hard time believing you have ADHD and misinterpreted your symptoms. For example, when Tonya told someone that she runs ADHD groups, the response was, "I'll tell you what the real diagnosis for ADHD is: lazy."

Our Experience

In running skills groups for adults with ADHD, we, the authors, know no one gains from misinterpretations of ADHD's symptoms as laziness or as simply a "deficiency." Between us, we have worked with individuals from all kinds of backgrounds. In his private practice, Greg currently runs ADHD groups specifically composed of lawyers and works one-on-one with athletes, artists, and high school, college, and graduate students as well as others diagnosed with ADHD. In 1994, while at Kaiser Permanente, Greg started the first-known HMO Adult ADHD group and ran this and other groups for Kaiser's Northwest Region (Oregon and Washington). Prior to retiring from Kaiser

Permanente, he mentored Tonya, who now runs ADHD and other groups at the Kaiser clinic where Greg could once be found. She's worked with teachers, carpenters, business owners, nurses, movie makers, college students, and activists, all with ADHD. Many of you, our readers, probably share their experience of being told, again and again, to try harder and be more motivated to change. This comes from the lopsided story of ADHD as all famine when really it's about feast and famine.

Re-seeing ADHD

More and more, ADHD experts acknowledge that ADHD has been wrongly seen as a deficit of attention (one side of the scale) and that it is really about difficulty *regulating*, or adjusting the scale. Regulating means adjusting to fit the situation and what you want out of it. We now know that ADHD's symptoms and remedies are about *adjusting* both your *attention* and your *actions*. ADHD is low attention and action regulation.

To grasp the idea of attention and action regulation, think of a car with a driver's seat and a passenger's seat. Regulation lets you be the driver. You turn your attention and action on, steer them where you want to go, keep them on the road you need to be on, and turn them off when you are finished with your drive. In this book, we describe strategies and skills that let you more often switch from the passenger's seat to the driver's. Try them and be convinced by your own experience.

As we redefine ADHD and what it means for you, we rely heavily on brain science, sticking close to it even when we describe our own ideas and experiences. We share what the science shows to be true at this time, even though scientific thought changes. After all, the alternative would be sharing what we or others simply hope, feel, or think to be true. We think we know what you'd prefer.

Along with the brain science, the interdisciplinary field of interpersonal neurobiology (IPNB) influences our ideas. IPNB sees your mind, brain, body, and social and environmental relationships as intimately connected, with a focus on using your mind and body to create optimal relationships and brains. We, too, see you as a complex combination of various elements and draw on multiple disciplines to illuminate how to use your attention and action to enhance your well-being. And when we know that we are pulling an idea from the field of IPNB, specifically from the work of Dr. Dan Siegel, we'll let you know.

Reading This Book

We want getting started to be as easy as possible. Our book's useless unless you read it, so start wherever you would like, at whichever chapter most intrigues you. Stick to whatever sections you find most useful. Our book map below lets you know the places available to visit. We hope that your first chapter will lead you to the others.

To get the most out of this book, we suggest that you get a journal for its practices of strategies and skills. You can think of it as your travel journal. Each time you visit a place (in other words, a chapter), you will have a chance to be a participant rather than just an observer. Your participation requires throwing yourself, again and again, into the practices you encounter. If you practice skills only once or twice, you may merely be ticking something off a to-do list, without accomplishing what brings you to this book. These skills can transform you, if you let them.

On Our Audience

We are writing to adults diagnosed with ADHD, so when we say "you" throughout this book, this is who we envision. At the same time, this book offers guidance to loved ones, teachers, managers, and mental health therapists who want to know more about you and what works as you try to move more often into the driver's seat of your attention and action.

Book Map

We share the latest research from various fields of study to move through the ways that we learn most effectively, to the ways relationships and environments influence us, to healthy habits and communication skills.

In chapter 1, Re-seeing ADHD, we give you an insider, behind-the-scenes look at ADHD. It's a look that comes from keeping up with the latest research and writings on ADHD by the scholars and scientists who plumb its depths.

Chapter 2 turns to Optimal Environments for Attention and Action Regulation. In this chapter, we describe ways to redesign your environments so they work with your brain instead of against it. We emphasize how to use the environment to guide your attention to where you need it to go and where you need it to linger, wherever you are and specifically at school, work, or home.

In chapter 3, we move from your external environments to your internal ones through Healthy Habits for Attention and Action Regulation. This chapter offers a fresh approach on how to influence your daily attention and behavior. We will examine the relationship of various healthy habits and practices, including the unique form of paying attention known as "mindfulness," to attention and action.

Chapter 4, Attachment and Attention, expands our focus to the foundation of your relationships, which affects what's happening both within and around you. Through suggested practices, you can discover insights into how you relate to others.

Chapter 5, Communication and Connection, turns to specific relationship skills. The chapter describes specific ways to connect to others and key communication rules such as:

- stop, look, and listen mindfully;

- paraphrase;

- describe; and

- stop burying the lead.

You will also learn how to pay attention to your audience when you're the speaker and how to "surf" urges to interrupt when you're the listener, riding the urge out as you would a wave rather than just acting on it.

We end with chapter 6, Overcoming Obstacles. This chapter presents common obstacles and what may be unexpected solutions to starting and sustaining your practice of skills and strategies.

Last Thoughts

You may be used to hearing that you need to change, that you need to "just do it" and figure it out, whatever your problem is. Instead of seeing you as a problem to be fixed, we see you as someone who can learn to work with your brain rather than against it. Experimenting with what works for you can increase your chances of getting what you want skillfully. We want to move you toward who and what matters to you.

CHAPTER 1

Re-seeing ADHD

If there's one line that captures the visible essence of ADHD, it may be John Medina's brain rule: "We don't pay attention to boring things" (2014, available at http://www.brainrules.net). We all look for the things that interest us, but having ADHD makes it hard to pay attention to anything but these things, leaving out a big part of life: bills, assignments for a class you hate, tasks at work you find tedious, paperwork, meetings, discussions that bore you, and so on. But what exactly *is* ADHD? Good question. Many have no idea. And those of us who have many ideas about the subject know that what we think we know will likely change. ADHD has proven to be much more complex than the view of it as a deficit of attention.

In this chapter, we share the latest understanding of ADHD, which has many scientists and scholars rethinking and redefining the disorder. You need to know the redefinition to understand how to change the things that bring you to this book. We then peek into your brain a little and look at how, despite what you may sometimes hear, your behavior makes sense. The chapter ends with how to use the knowledge about your brain and the world within which you live to create a life that you find meaningful. After all, what you do may make sense and still get you farther from what you really want.

What's the Problem, Exactly?

When it comes to mental health disorders, names reflect how the powers that be of the mental health field see them. And how they see ADHD and what's behind it keeps changing. Over the years, attention deficit/hyperactivity disorder (ADHD) has possessed many names, starting with "brain-injured child syndrome." The name gradually moved away from the idea of a defective brain, going from "minimal brain damage" to "minimal brain dysfunction" and then "hyperactive child syndrome" until 1980, when the mental health world renamed it "attention deficit disorder" (ADD) only to change this name, seven years later, to "attention-deficit hyperactivity disorder" (ADHD) (Matthews, Nigg, & Fair 2014). Although ADD no longer exists as an official diagnosis today, its use lingers. In 2013, the next official chance to rename the disorder passed, with the powers that be sticking with ADHD.

Yet, the biggest confusion about ADHD seems to stem from its reference to a "deficit." As ADHD scholars Hallowell and Ratey (2005) said, to refer to an attention "deficit" when speaking of the experience of ADHD "completely misses the point" (50). The attention is there. It often happens to cause problems when it insists on following the most immediate and interesting thoughts, events, and experiences while glossing over the boring, future-oriented ones, even when the person wishes otherwise. In a PBS *FRONTLINE* interview about children with ADHD, Russell Barkley pointed out that they "can pay attention to things that are around them in the immediate situation, so that it's really not an attention problem. What they don't pay attention to is what lies ahead in time, what has to be done next in order to get ready for the future" (*FRONTLINE* 2001). And as an adult with ADHD you have the same problem, which Barkley describes as a problem of *intention* instead of attention.

We describe ADHD attention as biased. Given the mental health field's own biases, the diagnostic criteria for ADHD highlight what your attention's biased against, what it moves away *from*. It's largely missing the other side of this—what your attention's biased toward, what it moves *to*. For example, your attention tends to move away from effortful activities or ones that require sustaining your attention and action for a prolonged period of time. Your attention moves away from the tedious, mundane, and repetitive. Translate this into such things as paying bills, checking the mail, organizing paperwork or physical spaces, writing essays, listening to detailed instructions, doing taxes, and keeping track of deadlines, and herein lies the part that leads to the disorder label. Because where your attention goes, your action follows. Procrastination and lack of follow-through with mundane things tend to lead to unwanted consequences. In diagnosing ADHD, the spotlight's fallen on where your attention's MIA and largely ignored where your attention can be found (see appendix B at the back of the book for the diagnostic criteria). The underfocus side has attracted more attention than the overfocus side of ADHD.

But here's the deal: concentrating on the underfocus side of ADHD and neglecting its overfocus counterpart lead to misunderstanding and misguided interventions. You need individuals, schools, counselors, and workplaces that understand the real nature of the "deficit" you experience. This means you need to understand it. The stakes are highest for you, and you may be your best advocate. After all, most people have no reason to know about ADHD until they know someone with it or find out that they themselves have it.

So what is the problem? Is it too little attention? Too little action? Too much attention or too much intention? Or is it too little or too much engagement and interest?

ADHD as Low Regulation

Understanding the real nature of ADHD starts with knowing its complexity and multiplicity. Many scientists see the label "ADHD" as a catchall for several similar conditions, just as cancer used to be seen as a single disease and we now know of many different kinds of cancer (e.g., Nigg, Karalunas, and Mitchell 2015). One of these conditions may be what Barkley (2014) proposes calling concentration deficit disorder, which at the moment carries the name sluggish cognitive tempo (SCT). It shares many of the symptoms of ADHD, but its outcomes and comorbidities (co-occurring disorders) appear to differ. The common denominator of SCT and other conditions labeled ADHD appears to be low attention and action regulation.

Remember John Medina's quote at the beginning of the chapter? Here it is, again: "We don't pay attention to boring things." Of course, the flip side of this is that we pay attention to interesting things. Both are true, but here's the thing. They are especially true when ADHD enters the picture. Without ADHD, you can make yourself pay attention to boring things and you can stop yourself from paying attention to interesting things when needed. With ADHD, you struggle. Really struggle. You follow your attention to your detriment and delight.

Acknowledging the preferential nature of ADHD attention, Lidia Zylowska, author of *The Mindfulness Prescription for Adult ADHD*, defines ADHD as "a deficit in attention regulation" (2012, 31). In doing so, she points out the same thing we do: that it's the flexibility, or control, of attention that's lacking rather than the attention itself.

But attention's tied to many things. Have you noticed that you struggle with staying motivated, following through with action, and controlling emotions? Russell Barkley explains these struggles by defining ADHD as a disorder of self-regulation, the ability to control your behavior and to stop and think before acting (Barkley 2012). Another ADHD scholar, Thomas Brown (2008), explains these struggles by describing ADHD as an executive function disorder. If your brain were a ship, your executive functions would be the powers of the ship's captain. With ADHD on board, the affected powers may include, as Dr. Brown describes them, prioritizing, organizing, and getting started on work; "focusing, sustaining and shifting attention to tasks"; regulating alertness, and keeping up one's effort and efficiency; "managing frustration and modulating emotions"; using working memory (to remember things that have just happened, such as where you put the keys) and being able to access what you know and have learned; and "monitoring and self-regulating action." All these executive functions can also translate into self-regulation abilities (Barkley 2012). Offering support for viewing ADHD as low self-regulation, German researchers recently conducted the first study to indicate substantially decreased ADHD symptoms among adults who learned to self-regulate through neurofeedback (NF) both at the end of 30 sessions of NF and six months later (Mayer, Blume, Wyckoff, Brokmeier, & Strehl 2015).

Along with Dr. Zylowska and Dr. Barkley (among others), we see ADHD as defined by low regulation. And, along with Dr. Barkley, we see ADHD as more than low *attention* regulation. But instead of redefining it as an all-encompassing self-regulation disorder, we see the value of focusing on two aspects of self: attention and action. After all, action encompasses emotions and motivation, and it's your actions (and inactions) that the world around you most clearly sees. Let's get to what's unseen that explains what's seen.

Brain Studies Expected to Shape the Future

Brain studies offer evidence of a biological basis for ADHD, and many scientists envision that doctors will one day use this evidence to help diagnose the disorder. Right now, diagnosis depends on behavioral evidence alone.

Brain studies also inform interventions, of course.

Your Attention and Action Biases: A Chemical Context

When boredom shows up, ADHD's extremes of forgetfulness, losing things, careless mistakes, distractibility, and disorganization come into full force. So does its extremes of excessive task-irrelevant activity and excessive giving up on tasks. When this happens, you need more than willpower to get your attention and energy back to where you need it. If, on the other hand, something of high interest or more immediate gratification appears, you need more than willpower to stop paying attention to it and to stop doing it. The opposing forces of under- and overfocus coexist with under- and overaction. And scientists think they're figuring out why.

Imagine a person unmoved by the mundane and highly sensitive to the immediate and interesting. Imagine that this person's brain lacked an essential chemical ingredient to motivate action and to find repetition and routine anything other than painfully boring. Now imagine that this person could turn up the level of this chemical—dopamine—through high-stimulation behavior. Would you expect that person to settle for a dull life or might you expect to see dopamine-triggering behaviors? You face these choices, according to the disrupted dopamine hypothesis of ADHD, which sees dopamine as one of the major contributors to your behaviors.

Dopamine's associated with many brain functions, including attention, arousal, and reward, and with ADHD, drug abuse, and Parkinson's disease (Anderson 2013). It's often misidentified as a pleasure chemical because it promises pleasure and other rewards (McGonigal 2013), and the promise of reward motivates attention and action (even if reality fails to deliver what's promised). In one word, dopamine equals *wanting* (van den Bos and de Ridder 2006). Studies show that, at specific locations, the brains of people with ADHD release too little dopamine or release and reload it too quickly, cutting short the communication between neurons. According to the disrupted dopamine pathway theory, then, your low attention and action regulation starts with disrupted dopamine reward pathways, decreasing your available dopamine at the level of your synapses (where your neurons communicate with each other).

Low attention and action regulation makes sense if you lack dopamine in certain areas to tell your brain that ordinary, routine things will be worth your attention and action. Backing up the disrupted dopamine theory, brain studies show that the brains of adults with, versus without, ADHD have overall lower dopamine levels at certain dopamine D1 and D2 receptors (e.g., Volkow et al. 2009, 2011). Differences show up with some other chemicals too, but, by far, dopamine's received the most attention. Researchers have even proposed genotyping for low dopamine function as a way to diagnose ADHD more accurately (Gold et al. 2014).

The findings on low dopamine function and ADHD offer a possible explanation for your behaviors. If the dopamine dysfunction hypothesis is true, it clarifies your biases toward the interesting and immediate. It sheds light on the decreased capacity to delay gratification that's consistently found with

ADHD (Jackson and Mackillop 2016). It also makes sense of the high rate of novelty seeking seen with ADHD (e.g., Donfranceso et al. 2015) and increased risk of early death associated with higher rates of injury, accidents, and health-risking behaviors (see Barkley 2016). Seeking what's exciting and interesting, what evokes your emotions, what's novel and what's immediately gratifying are all ways to trigger dopamine. Doing what you can to increase available dopamine makes sense as a strategy to motivate attention and action when your brain, for all practical purposes, shuts down otherwise. As Gold et al. (2014) put it, low dopamine function leads to behaviors to compensate for dopamine deficiency. In fact, Nora D. Volkow, Director of the National Institute on Drug Abuse, told an interviewer that given the findings on lower levels of dopamine, she'd describe ADHD as a disruption of interest that requires tasks to be made more engaging (Reinberg 2009).

These dopamine findings put something else into perspective: forgetfulness and losing things. Working memory, your ability to hold onto thoughts and to juggle them short-term, depends on dopamine neurotransmission, with dopamine D1 receptors playing a large role (McNab et al. 2009). And guess what else depends on remembering things? Action regulation. How can you start actions—say, paying a bill—unless you remember what you need to do or are reminded of it?

Everything is caused. Sometimes we're aware of the causes of actions and events and sometimes awareness gives us an opportunity to choose what we accept and what we change. Our hope is that you'll use the knowledge about your brain's biochemistry, specifically the connection between dopamine and your behavior, to your advantage. Of course, dopamine interacts with other brain chemicals and factors but there's no need to know about all these interactions to identify paths that are friendly to your particular brain.

As we chart brain-friendly paths, we'll look wide—across the lifespan. And we'll look deep—into gene–environment interactions. To date, only one of these gene–environment pathways is known: it's childhood lead exposure combined with possessing the mutation of a particular gene that helps control lead's effects (Nigg et al. 2015). We also delve some into your early years because, to date, only two studies appear to challenge current understanding of adult ADHD as starting during childhood by suggesting that sometimes it may start during adulthood (Caye et al. 2016; Moffitt et al. 2015).

Adapting Your Attention and Action to Your Reality

What does low attention and action regulation look like? Carrie's story shows us.

> Carrie worked as a much sought-after business consultant and suffered financial difficulties. Despite working full-time and at a high wage, she ultimately earned very little due to lack of sending clients bills for services rendered. She described billing as an afterthought and thought it could wait. Except she kept it waiting and waiting. She partly put off billing because of her office space. Paperwork, objects, and boxes lay scattered throughout the room. She was unable to see any uncovered surface, on table or floor. The disorganization also interfered with her ability to be on time with delivering work promised. Clients, however, kept coming to her because of her significant talent.
>
> Carrie was on ADHD medication which helped her focus. What to focus on was still up to her. She found her consulting work exciting and she went straight to it on weekdays. What she set aside, day after day, was the tedious work of daily planning, filing receipts, sending bills to clients, and also paying her own bills. Over a few months, she had accumulated hundreds of dollars of late

fees. Absorbed by the excitement of her work, she hardly knew what day of the week it was.

On the one hand, Carrie could hyper-focus on talking to clients and surfing online, losing track of time. On the other, she could barely tolerate attending to the mountain of mundane tasks piling up. Despite repeated negative consequences of her selective attention, she found it nearly impossible to rally her efforts to the activity of billing and organizing. Her failure to get paid for her work threatened her ability to continue it.

In reading about Carrie, you may have noticed that she was plenty active and plenty attentive. What she needed help with was balancing her attention and action so that she could sustain the life that she wanted to be living. She needed to learn how to shift some of her focus and energy from what excited and interested her to what bored and even frustrated her. Carrie needed attention and action regulation skills. Unless your reality includes a personal assistant, you, too, need these skills to adapt to the demands of bills, mail, distractions, work tasks, and so on. Even if you had a personal assistant, you would need these skills to direct the assistant.

The Four S's of Attention and Action Regulation

Attention and action regulation involves four behaviors. You can remember them as "the four S's":

- Starting,

- Sustaining,

- Stopping, and

- Shifting.

Let's look at what this means for attention (remember we will focus our words on attention because of the overlap between attention and action). You need to *start* your attention on a task when it wants to soar elsewhere, *sustain* it when you need it to stay, *stop* it when you need to switch to another task, and then *shift* it where you need it to go next. Psychologist Rick Hanson, PhD (2015) points out that regulating your attention, which he defines as "becoming more able to place it where you want it and keep it there, and more able to pull it away from what's bothersome or pointless...is the foundation of changing your brain, and thus your life, for the better." It looks like this: I say I'm going to go online for just five minutes and when I see five minutes have passed, I *stop*. I then *shift* my attention back to my work, telling myself, "I need to get to work now." Next I *start* getting to work and *sustain* my attention and action on it. In this book, when we say "low attention and action regulation" we are talking about ADHD. "ADHD" as a label just less accurately describes what science shows us it really is: variations of low attention and action regulation.

Ready to start regulating? Let's begin with understanding both sides of your attention.

KNOW THYSELF 1: What Attracts Your Attention?

For one week, get to know what *starts* and *sustains* your attention. What are you doing when you can focus? You may even hyper-focus on these things or give them a degree of attention that interferes with other areas of your life (such as getting home on time, or listening to someone close to you). These will likely be your high-interest activities. Write or draw them into your journal. Snap pictures of them, if you want, to paste into your journal. Do what works to sustain your interest.

Get to know as well what repels your attention. Where is it hard for you to start and sustain your attention and action? You'll know these things by looking at what you procrastinate or avoid. These will likely be your low-interest activities. Now add these to your journal.

If you're unsure how to notice your attention's favoritism, then notice what you do from day to day. If we watched you for a few days, what would we see you doing for much of your time? Or again and again? These things are likely your higher-interest activities. What would we see you avoiding or putting off doing? These are likely your lower-interest activities.

Hint: For help with this, you can ask someone close to you and non-judgmental to tell you what he or she has noticed about your attention. You can write or draw your answers, whichever you prefer.

When ready, get out your journal again, and create a list using the categories below with up to seven lines or spaces (seven will be easier to remember than a longer list). The first three lines may look like this:

Higher-interest activities (easy for me to pay attention to)

- Reading the news and blogs online
- Attending group therapy meetings
- Swimming

Lower-interest activities (hard for me to pay attention to)

- Going to post office to mail off package
- Arranging doggy daycare
- Putting away my piles of clothes

Write down how many hours and minutes you pay attention to each activity over the course of each day (you may need to keep a log of this for a day to be accurate).

Look at the data you've collected. Do you see any places where you'd like to shift attention, to give more attention to one thing (such as going through mail) and less attention to another (such as games on your phone)? You probably found some imbalanced attention (and action).

So now you may be wondering: What can you do about your imbalanced attention? First, let's be clear, you *can* do something. Brain science has shown us that our brains develop until we die. Scientists and scholars refer to the creation of new neurons as *neurogenesis* and call the brain's perpetual ability to change due to various factors *neuroplasticity*. What does this mean for you? You have a reason to be hopeful. You can strengthen your brain's ability to regulate your attention and action.

Now that you see where your attention goes, we can look at one way to balance your attention, when you need it. Let's start with the context of trying to learn something. We'll start with optimal ways to learn. Then we'll look at how to apply them to pay attention to what you are trying to learn when it's challenging. You will then have a chance to practice with *Challenge Thyself 1*: High-Low Exercise.

Knowing How We Learn Matters for Paying Attention

In the 1980s, a Harvard psychologist, Howard Gardner, published a book describing seven distinct forms of intelligence. Almost three decades later, developmental molecular biologist John Medina suggested that the number of categories of intelligence may exceed seven billion (about the population of the world). Despite this difference of estimation, the two scholars agree on this: our brains are different.

Because our brains are different and there are different forms of intelligence, many have asked whether it makes sense to figure out our own unique way(s) of learning and learn through these ways. Many who ask this question refer to "learning styles." What the research shows is that instead of being about "styles," learning is about multiples: multiple ways to access content (Hattie 2011) and multiple ways to show your knowledge and skills (Darling-Hammond 2010). The most effective way to learn appears to be through multiple contexts and multiple senses. For instance, you might learn about fractions through cooking and through musical notes, which include eighth notes, quarter notes, and half notes. (See http://www.edutopia.org.) Want to remember what you are reading? Pair it with visuals. Pair it with sound. Pair it with smell. When you learn by doing something (instead of just reading, watching, or hearing about it), you are likely pairing what you are learning with various senses. Create a multisensory environment for learning and you're likely to remember more now and years later (see http://www.brainrules.net/sensory-integration). In 2015, NPR interviewed a teacher who did exactly this, using various materials (colored paper, flowerpot, garbage can, tape, spaghetti), activities (drawing, coloring, cutting, singing), and contexts (speed dating, puzzles) to teach her students math (Turner 2015).

As you practice strategies and skills from this book, remember multiples, especially if you get stuck. Practice the book's exercises under different circumstances and using multiple senses. Other than increasing your learning, using multiples can give you the variety and change you need to stay interested. And you need to be interested to pay attention (Horvath, Herleman, & McKie 2006).

It's harder to learn something effortful and repetitious with low attention and action regulation, so let's look at how you can combine the science of learning and attention to increase focus and performance. Remember the problem: so much of what requires your attention bores you. How can you trigger dopamine for *these* things? Borrow dopamine from other things. The things that excite and stimulate you, your high-interest activities that trigger your dopamine, all share something. They promise reward (McGonigal 2013).

Dopamine's what's released when we anticipate pleasure and all things we find rewarding. Sex, drugs, and food trigger dopamine. If you are willing to put a lot of effort into getting something, again and again, with no obligation to get it, it likely triggers dopamine. Notice that we said it's released when we *anticipate* pleasure and when we face the *promise* of reward. Whether we actually achieve pleasure or another anticipated reward is another matter. (Vegas, anyone?) So to motivate action, you just need to expect a reward, or the possibility of one. And you can see where this is the case for you. This is where your *Know Thyself 1* exercise comes into play. If you skipped over it, pause and go back to it before continuing so you can use the next practice.

Once you know your high-interest activities and your low-interest ones, you have set the stage for a dopamine transfer. When faced with something that bores you or that you find highly effortful—your procrastinated low-interest activities—integrate your high-interest activities. That is, inject their dopamine-triggering qualities into your low-interest activities. Dr. McGonigal (2013) calls this "dopaminizing." Remember, too, that with dopaminizing you are also getting the dopamine-triggering novelty of the combination of high- and low-interest activities. And when you apply the rule of multiples (multiple contexts and multiple senses), you can increase your learning for both your low-interest activities and how to dopaminize them.

Let's look at two examples.

• *Lyrical Lynn*

Lynn, a lawyer, diagnosed with ADHD and on ADHD medication, had failed the bar exam of the state where she currently lived. It was an oral exam requiring memorization of laws. She had passed a different state's bar exam easily.

It was a multiple-choice exam, and Lynn reported that it was easy to pass when she could see the answers. As she prepared for the oral exam, however, she struggled with concentrating and remembering how to recite the laws. She said her brain shut down when she tried to memorize. She noticed her self-esteem dropping and felt herself becoming discouraged. She felt ready to give up.

Lynn sought help from a mental health therapist who explored Lynn's strengths and interests as she prepared for the oral bar exam. Through this exploration, Lynn recalled her musical abilities and how she had used music to enhance her learning throughout school and college by putting class content to song when she needed to memorize it. Feeling ashamed of her "need" to do this, she had kept it private. Lynn's therapist encouraged her in doing what worked, and Lynn studied for her oral exam by converting laws into songs. This conversion increased her ability to focus on the laws and increased her confidence. She passed her oral exam with raving responses.

• Math-Moving Mitch

Mitch, who'd been diagnosed with ADHD as an adult, hated math. He had a hard time focusing whenever he tried to study it and whenever his teachers taught it. After flunking his college algebra course multiple times, he met with a mental health therapist to see whether his ADHD was coming between him and college graduation. The therapist got to know Mitch and asked him about his interests. An avid basketball fan, Mitch's favorite thing to do was watch his city's basketball team play. He could do this for hours. His therapist asked him about his favorite position. It was point guard. Mitch agreed to try to be a math point guard. Moving numbers around on a *whiteboard (and moving his body as he did so), Mitch solved equations such as $3/10 = 7/x$, as follows. Mitch s aw x as a player that needed to score, the top numbers as players at the front court, and the bottom numbers as players at the back court. As a point guard, he knew he had to get x to the front court and open so x could shoot the ball. So first he moved x to the front court and had $3x/10 = 7$. Then he had to get x free and unblocked by player 3, the player sticking closest to x at the moment. This meant moving 10, which was still at the back court, to the front court to help x out (10 was on x's team because they both started at the back court). When 10 moved over to the front court, he had $3x = 7*10$, or $3x = 70$. Now, x just had to get free of player 3 to score, which he did with $x = 70/3$. By looking at numbers as players he had to direct on a whiteboard representation of a basketball court, Mitch passed his math course with an A.*

Lynn and Mitch effectively got what they wanted by skillfully infusing a low-interest, highly effortful activity with a high-interest one and stimulating multiple senses. Lynn sang law to memorize it, adding audio to visual. Mitch saw and moved math, using the context of basketball to create a multisensory environment combining vision, touch, and proprioception (data from various senses that tell you the position, motion, and balance of your body). Lynn and Mitch turned learning law and math into more attractive ventures by trying a novel, higher-interest way of learning them, with the promise of immediate reward—the fun of singing for one and the chance to play point guard for the other.

What about you? We learn way more by doing than by just reading or hearing about something, so here's your chance to practice.

CHALLENGE THYSELF 1: High-Low Exercise

How can you use your areas of high interest to start and sustain attention for low-interest activities that you are trying to learn? Write or draw your high-interest and low-interest activities/subjects into your regulation skills practice journal. Create a list with up to seven lines for each side. Here's an example of three per side:

Low-interest activities/ subjects	High-interest activities/ subjects
paying bills	cooking
cleaning the bathroom	checking Facebook
organizing paperwork	socializing with friends/family
writing	history

Pick something of low interest to you that you are trying to learn (facts, a task or skill) and where you'd like to increase your focus. Now draw a line from it to something of high interest.

> ***Example:*** paying bills ➔ checking Facebook

In your journal, brainstorm alone or with someone about how to incorporate the activity on the right into the activity on the left, to make it more interesting to you. Brainstorming consists of coming up with as many novel ideas as you can about something. You want as many fresh ideas as possible about how to integrate your high- and low-interest activities.

- **Brainstorming rule #1:** Welcome all ideas. No idea's too crazy or unrealistic. Just start by letting the ideas come without judging them. Leave them alone to start. You can evaluate them later.

- **Brainstorming rule #2:** Write down or draw all the ideas and keep putting them down on paper until you come up with no other ideas. You can also put your ideas on a whiteboard. The point is to make them visual. If you have exhausted all ideas at the moment and come up with other ideas later, add them later.

Example: Here's our initial brainstorming of ideas for integrating Facebook and bill-paying:

1. Post on Facebook about bill-paying avoidance and ask for ideas, support, and accountability (you can choose one or all friends for this and post a day and time when you will pay bills so they can cheer you on).

2. Start a bill-paying group on Facebook of others who would like to share when they have bills due and when they have paid them so that all members receive cheerleading and praise when they pay bills.

3. Invite Facebook friends to an online or face-to-face bill-paying party each month (different friends can be the host each month).

4. Invite friends to a one-time bill-paying party where everyone sets up automatic payments and gets help with this, if needed.

5. Each time you pay a bill, reward yourself with ten minutes of Facebook time.

In the bills-Facebook example, integrating a high-interest activity and a low-interest one puts the impersonal activity of bill paying into a relational context, yielding a *multicontextual* experience.

To integrate a high-interest activity and a low-interest one while creating a *multisensory* experience, envision how you could stimulate at least two of your senses—sight, sound, touch, taste, smell, and proprioception.

Here's an example of stimulating sight and sound for a high-interest activity of music combined with a low-interest activity of checking one's planner (the next chapter has more on planners):

Use a planner with events organized like a song and/or duration of event marked by quarter, half, and whole notes;

Make the planner sing by attaching a singing greeting card to the outside of a physical planner and/or have your electronic planner timed to play a recorded voice singing what you need to do at that time.

When you have finished brainstorming ideas for your high-low exercise, the next part of brainstorming is evaluation. Look at your ideas. Which ideas are realistic means to what you want to happen? Which would work and are possible to put into action? Keep these and prioritize them, giving highest priority to the one that has the highest likelihood of working and being possible to put into action. Now choose the first and perhaps second idea from your priority list. If you'd like, look at the pros and cons for the top two ideas to guide your choice of which one to start with. The final step of brainstorming is to put your ideas into action and evaluate the results.

When you evaluate the results, consider the first two S's of the four S's of regulation. Does your idea work to 1) start attention and action and 2) sustain them? If no, look at whether you can change something to move closer to yes. For example, some of our ADHD group members have said they tried to practice a high-low combination and a spouse interrupted the practice. This requires some problem solving. A spouse will perhaps dislike the music you've chosen to dopaminize work around the house. Rather than giving up on the music-chore mix, you may have to change how you listen to the music (such as wearing headphones), your timing (such as waiting until your spouse is out), or your music choice to one you find dopaminizing and your spouse finds tolerable. Of course, it's also possible that when you say no to questions one and two above, you need to try a different idea on your brainstorming list. Remember the brainstorming list for the Facebook-bill combination? If you chose to try rewarding each bill paid with ten minutes of Facebook and discovered that this turned into 100 minutes per bill even when you had to get up and go across the room to turn off an alarm, trying a different idea on the list, such as the one-time party to set up automatic payments, may make sense.

If the high-low exercise sounds like play that's useful, we're glad. We learn from play. If you see this as useless play, are you willing to experiment? We learn through testing things out. We learn from the freedom to explore and succeed or fail. As John Medina (2014) notes, Google knows this. Google encourages employees to use 20% of their time for exploration. This 20% exploration time has led to 50% of Google's new products, including Gmail and Google News. What could it offer you?

As we introduce more and more skills and strategies, continue to look at ways to turn up your interest level, to keep practicing this particular skill of integrating high- and low-interest activities. We will try to help by offering suggestions for how to do this along the way. Remember, acquiring skills requires practice, practice, practice, and more practice.

The Road Ahead

We are more than our actions. Our physical and interpersonal environments, past and present, influence us and our attention and action control. In fact, environments, particularly our early ones, may better explain the rise of ADHD over recent years than genetic factors (Christakis 2016). As we look at ways to increase your attention and action regulation, we give your environments a lot of attention. In chapter 4, we even turn some attention to your earliest environments.

Key Points from Chapter 1

- With ADHD, it's what you do with your attention that tends to get you into trouble. Often you are doing different things than you need to be doing at the moment. ADHD is better understood as an attention and action regulation disorder than as a deficit of attention. What you need are action and attention regulation skills.

- Attention and action regulation involves the four S's: starting, sustaining, stopping, and shifting. In this chapter, we focused on the first two.

- Using *Know Thyself 1*, see where your attention goes (with ADHD, there appears to be decreased awareness of this, so it's a helpful starting place) and what your attention avoids.

- With *Challenge Thyself 1*, engage your attention and action by using your high-interest activities to rev up low-interest ones.

CHAPTER 2

Optimal Environments for Attention and Action Regulation

Have you ever heard of global warming? We thought so. We often hear about the effects we have on our environment. In this chapter, we will look at the effects that your environment has on *you* and, specifically, your attention and action regulation. Here, we want to delve into physical environments, whether these are at work, school, or home. (In subsequent chapters, we look at optimal social relationships for self-regulation.) We'll start with an overview of why our physical environments matter for us all. Then we'll talk about why the elements of the immediate physical environment especially matter when you struggle with attention and action regulation. Finally, of course, we'll help you redesign your physical environment to work with, instead of against, your attention and intention.

Environments Matter

Let's time-travel back to late 1700s Italy. There, an Italian scientist, Michele Vincenzo Giacinto Malacarne, determined the destinies of two birds from the same clutch of eggs and of two canine littermates. One bird and dog got lucky. They were brought up within enriched environments with activities. Their unlucky siblings were destined to impoverished, isolated environments without activities. Whatever their luck, the animals later had their lives "sacrificed" so that their brains could be examined for science. Guess what Malacarne found? "Enriched" animals had larger brains. Before you scoff, realize that this was the first time that experimentation indicated that our cerebral development depends on experience. We now call this "neuroplasticity."

Centuries passed before scientists conducted the first go-to study on neuroplasticity. They examined the brains of rats placed into enriched versus impoverished environments. One group received social contact, toys, and maze training. The other group received none of these or much of anything except what they needed to stay alive. The scientists found that the cerebral cortices of the enriched rats weighed more and showed increased thickness and neural activity compared to the cerebral cortices of the impoverished rats.

Research on humans suggests similar results. In 1993, for example, researchers obtained brain tissue from individuals who had, before their deaths, agreed to donate their brains to science. The researchers looked at a particular area of the cerebral cortex controlling word understanding. Comparing this area from individuals who had a college education to those who had only a high school education, they found that the brains of the college educated showed evidence of greater neural activity (Jacobs, Schall, & Scheibel 1993).

For better or worse, experiences and environments change the brain. Lucky for you, you have some power when it comes to your experiences and environments. No one can just put you into a cage and deprive you of social contact and stimulation... well, unless you go to prison and are placed into isolation. So let's say that most of us have power. You'll really only know this, though, if you exercise it.

Redesigning Environments: Distractions and Guides

Rather than being deprived of stimulation like the unlucky animals of the research we described, you likely have choices— and a lot of them—about where to place your attention and action. Indeed, all the choices can be the problem. It's easy to become overwhelmed and turn to the same choices, again and again, even if these choices get you into trouble. Does it ever seem like your stimuli-enriched environment and your I-do-what-I-want attention are colluding to keep your attention away from where it needs to be? Well, they are. This means you have to become an interior designer of sorts. You need to design your environments knowing the workings of your interior.

Your attention (interior) wants to pay attention to what's happening right now that's exciting. So when it comes to doing something boring with no immediate reward, such as saving money for a house, it gets hard for you to remember to save when you want to spend, especially when you see something you really want right now. The yank to spend simply overpowers the tug to save. And if you stop yourself from making one purchase by remembering your long-term goal of buying a house, another even more desirable thing might come along, and you're back to spending again. What can you do? Design your exterior environment to work with your interior. When it comes to long-term goals, this may mean introducing representations of your desired future into your present by, for example, taping pictures of your desired home on your computer screen if your impulsive purchases primarily occur online. The point is to recognize your brain's biases as you design your environment to keep you on the paths you want to follow.

We'll give you practice redesigning your environment and seeing what works for you. Remember, you may have to try a variety of designs to find the ones that work. We'll start by giving you the big picture of what your design needs to have and then narrowing this down to specifics for you to try.

Regulating your attention (starting, sustaining, stopping, and shifting) means controlling your environment. It's a technique called "stimulus control." Masters of self-control master their environments to master themselves. They know the power of temptations to get them off their desired path and they know the power of signposts and other guides to keep them on it. It's those who fail to recognize the power of the environment who are most apt to lose control.

Your environment must contain cues, prompts, and reminders that guide your attention to where you need it and exclude distractions that tempt your attention away. Barkley (2012) describes engineering your environment to contain cues, prompts, and reminders for your attention and action as *externalizing* what is internally weak. We call these cues and reminders "guiding lights" and distractions "flashing lights." Think of the guiding lights as the reliable lights of lighthouses and think of the flashing lights as the blinking bright lights of a big city billboard. The first urges, "This way" and the second screams, "Look at me!"

Let's start by looking at your flashing lights, using the exercise below. For now, look at your flashing lights for only one environment, such as work, school, or home. Have you picked an environment? Now we'll look at your flashing lights there. Remember to get your journal for the book's practices. (Or download the worksheet version of this exercise that's available at http://www.newharbinger.com/34459.)

KNOW THYSELF 2: Creating a Pro–Attention- and Action-Regulating Environment

Part 1: *Flashing Lights*

Pick an environment (school, work, home).

Environment: _____

Example: home when I need to work on a task on the computer

    In this context/environment, what pulls your attention away from where you need it? For ideas, think about what pulls your eyes, ears, and body away. List no more than seven of these.

My Flashing Lights: _____

Example: relative's requests to do chores, dog whining for me because I'm his favorite

Other possible examples: Text message/e-mail alerts on phone or computer; phone calls; visitors (coworkers, family, friends, strangers, neighbors); television; websites (surfing); pets; wandering mind; passersby (seen/heard through window/door).

Part 2: *Guiding Lights*

Now, for this same environment, what guides or could guide your attention to where you need it?

My Guiding Lights: _____

Example: posted task list

Other examples (all practical ways to regulate attention and activity): use of appealing physical cues, posting signs related to work or school rules, recorded or timed reminders to start/stop, stay on task, or pause for a break.

Part 3: *Replacement*

How you can replace your flashing lights with guiding lights?

Ways I can replace my flashing lights with guiding ones:

Example: Close self into room where I am less accessible to dog and relative or work away from home at library or café. Wear headphones playing music, if useful. Tape assignment task list to the side of computer monitor where I can see it as I work.

Effectiveness Hint 1: You need to remove flashing lights from your field of attention. Sometimes this means having your flashing lights out of sight *and* reach. If your phone's your distraction, and you put it into your pocket, you may pull it out of your pocket without realizing.

Effectiveness Hint 2: Avoid replacing one distracting environment with another. If you go to the library to work and the detective novels or magazines pull your attention away from your work, go somewhere else.

Effectiveness Hint 3: It may help to be sure that your loved ones know your plans and are onboard. (We'd hate to get you into trouble.)

If this practice leaves you overwhelmed, work only on part 1 for now. Just removing your flashing lights can greatly increase your ability to focus. You can come back to the other parts of the practice later, if needed.

Let's now look at how this exercise works for different environments: school, work, home, and relationships. We'll start with school. Much of what we say about attention and action regulation at school applies to the other environments. So if you're more concerned about what happens at work and home, it's still helpful to start with the school example below. There's no need to be attending school to learn from the school example.

School

As a student, you need to pay attention to lessons while at school. This is necessary—and it's insufficient. You also need to show what you know via tests and homework assignments. Attention and action regulation matters for both. Knowing the two sides of your attention, what's the first and perhaps the easiest thing you can do to increase your ability to regulate it? Choose high-interest courses over low-interest ones, if possible. This is a start and, again, only a start. You're likely to find that you struggle with paying attention some of the time even to subjects of high interest (for example, when someone lectures on them). What else can you do? Reach out to your school for accommodations. Accommodations—modifications and adjustments that enable performance—include a quiet environment where you are alone to work on exams; more time for exams; the option of oral exams instead of written ones; and early access to homework assignments. You have a right to accommodations and can find an empathetic community of others who get you. In fact, you can collaborate with your school on the attention regulation exercises below.

Let's use some of the strategies from *Know Thyself 2*. Remember your journal.

FLASHING LIGHTS

Whatever the situation where you want to increase your attention regulation, start with flashing lights that draw your attention away from where you need it to be. What are these likely to be at school? Here's a real example of these. This one is of Tonya's husband, with his permission (as long as we mention that he's very handsome).

• *Study-Shuffling Sergio*

Prior to being diagnosed with ADHD, Sergio started his MBA. He started with high test scores and high hopes. By the end of his second term, he faced academic probation. What happened? He skipped school—mentally. His body was there while his mind was somewhere else. He struggled with a long list of flashing lights. When he had Internet and his computer, he read CNN and online newspapers during class. (If a professor came up behind him, he had classwork a click away.) If he unexpectedly lost Internet connection, he focused his energy on trying to find a way to reconnect, all the while missing the lectures. When he had to be offline for a particular class (because it had no online access), he played games on his phone and worked on his calendar. He also brought work from a part-time job to class. When studying became urgent, he brought textbooks and used the class time for one course to study for another course. If he had none of these distractions, sometimes his thoughts obliged him. During the World Cup, one of his super high-interest events, all he could think about during class was when he would watch the next match.

As he sped toward academic probation, Sergio could see it coming and became increasingly anxious. He knew he had to leave his distractions at home, but he kept bringing them. Why? Because each time his distractions pulled his attention away, he told himself, "That was the last time." His road to academic probation was paved with "last times" and good intentions. Do you see his flashing lights? They include the Internet, phone, unrelated work materials, unrelated textbooks, and thoughts of a high-interest event.

Do you struggle with any of the same flashing lights as Sergio? Now stop and open your journal to *Know Thyself 2* and add any flashing lights that you share with him. Then add any other flashing lights still missing from your list, if they apply. These could be such things as friends, classmates, and sights outside a window. If you want to go only as far as part 1 of the exercise, the part on removing flashing lights, then remove these flashing lights from your field of vision when needed. For Sergio, he needed his flashing lights removed both when he was attending class and when he was studying. In chapter 3, we address interior distractions. For now, we are focusing on exterior ones.

For Sergio, removal of flashing lights meant that he had to leave his computer, phone, and unrelated job and school materials at home or inside a locker at school when he went to class. And he had to stop saying that tomorrow would be different than today and yesterday. He had to acknowledge that if he brought his distractions with him, each day would be like the previous 180 days he thought would be different.

Before we move on to guiding lights, be sure you've given yourself time to work on reducing your flashing lights. Notice what happens with your attention and action when your flashing lights are out of sight (and hearing and reach).

Next, we give an example of guiding lights at school. Again, these guiding lights may be the same ones that you need at work and home. If you want to try the guiding lights part of *Know Thyself 2*, please read on.

GUIDING LIGHTS

At school, you need lights that guide your attention to your studies, both inside and outside class. Think of each course you have as a plane. Think of your attention as a runway. You need to know which plane needs to be on the runway and when. In airports, ground controllers working with air-traffic controllers guide planes to the runway when it's the right time for each, whether they are arriving or departing. And they clear only one plane at a time to take off or land. Otherwise, accidents occur. Accidents would also occur if pilots were distracted from listening to the controllers by the flashing lights of other planes. Guiding lights act as your controllers, and include tools like planners and reminders on your phone. They tell you when a particular course needs to arrive and depart the runway of your attention.

Guide 1: Planners. With few exceptions, you need one and only one planner. If you must have a work-specific planner, you still need only one for everything else. It can be paper or digital. It just needs to be:

- easy to carry,

- quick to access,

- simple to use and edit (if you have to write tiny letters and are unable to read them later, it's out), and

- noticeable (so you remember to use it!).

This means you may have to try out a few. And notice what's missing from the list: perfect. Aim for effective instead. Feel free to use your creativity to make your planner effective. Greg has seen members of his groups attach motion detectors to their planners so that when they walked by, the planners moved, sang, or released a pop-up design, also attached. These planners got their attention!

What goes into your planner? For school, it will be the days and times you have to attend classes and your homework time for each course (whether the homework means a specific assignment or just studying). You also must revise your planner according to how often these things change. For example, although you may be able to put your course schedule into your planner for the entire length of the course (anywhere from 10 to 17 weeks), you likely need to add homework into your planner weekly or daily.

Planner Entries	Friday May 27th	Saturday May 28th
9 a.m.	revise three stories	exercise
10 a.m.	meeting with writing group	family story time at library
11 a.m.	meeting with writing group	
Noon	lunch	lunch

And here's something else: planners are about more than due dates. Once you know the due date for an assignment, work back from there to the days and times you need to work on the assignment to meet the due date. Want to know about an accommodation you may be able to obtain? Knowing due dates ahead of other students. Yes, you can request this "heads-up" as an accommodation so that you have more time to plan for, and work on, assignments. Another accommodation you may be able to obtain is getting oral versus written assignments and tests. The place to go at your school for accommodations may be called something like the "accessible education center."

You may be saying it's all fine and good to have a planner but your trouble is getting yourself to actually log things into it. Remember the exercises from chapter 1? The examples at the end of *Challenge Thyself 1* suggested a way to combine a love of music with using your planner, what Greg calls "making your planner sing to you." Another way you can turn up the fun of using your planner is through rewarding yourself for logging into it. You can, for example, find stickers you really like and keep them at the back of your planner to put next to activities and events when you log them. An immediate reward! Ditto for when you finish what's logged.

Guide 2: Cues. Our brains are association machines. How can you get your brain to associate certain cues with logging into and checking your planner? With homework time? Be regular. Routines and rituals are brain reminders. So have a specific time and environment that tell your brain it's planner time. The most effective planner times are when you start your day, so you can check what's ahead, and when you end it, so you can log what you need to carry over into the next day and plan for the next day. A midday planner time also reminds you of what's there and lets you adjust your schedule, if needed. If you have only one time of day to work on your planner, pick one that will most easily allow consistency. Consistency = routine = brain cue. If you choose a morning time, your brain will associate mornings with logging into and checking your planner. If you consistently work on your planner when you have your morning coffee, your brain will also associate your morning coffee with your planner.

Let's look at another example of cueing: homework and study time. This could mean you have a desk for homework and studying. Whenever you sit at this desk, you do schoolwork and only schoolwork. Your brain then turns the desk into a cue for schoolwork—just as when you sit at the wheel of your car, your brain knows you are there to drive instead of knit. If you consistently study for a course as soon as class lets out, the end of the class also becomes a cue for studying. Other cues include posted signs and physically appealing stimuli, such as colors. For example, when you add things to your planner, you could choose colors you really like to highlight different courses. Or choose ones that you already associate with something, such as green for a course on money. These colors then become cues for the courses. Colors are one kind of visual. Medina (2014) notes that we have twice as much recognition for pictures versus text, so can you think of any pictures you can use? You can create or download images or use stickers, for example.

Cueing lets your brain do what it does so that remembering becomes more effortless. Your brain says, "I've got this." Just be sure it's saying this days before homework's due rather than the day of (that is, avoid cueing your brain to say, "Homework time!" each Wednesday morning for a Wednesday course that starts at noon).

Finally, if you need a cue for paying attention to time, one of the best ones to have is a watch. Keep reading for more on using a watch.

Guide 3: Timers. Designate how much time you'll work on a particular course and a particular project for it. Use the designated time for this course only. If you're likely to lose track of time, start a timer, whether it's a timer on an electronic device, an old-fashioned kitchen timer, or an actual hourglass. Choose one with a sound and appearance you find pleasant to increase the chances you'll use it.

Guide 4: Alarms. Related to timers are alarms. Timers tell you how much time you have left and may have an alarm to tell you it's time to stop. Alarms tell you when to go, start, or pause for a break. This means you need to set alarms to tell you when to shift your attention to getting to your classes and when you need to shift your attention to starting homework. You can set these alarms each weekend for the upcoming week of school as you add classes and homework into your planner. Planning for the future can be really hard for you. Try out setting alarms for future events with patience, knowing that you need practice, practice, practice to work out the kinks and become more comfortable with it.

Speaking of alarms, there's another sound that can work as a guiding light: one that comes at random intervals and is a cue for you to stop and ask, "Am I on task?" If you are on task, you have a chance to give yourself a little reward. Otherwise, you have a chance to get back on task rather than to stay off task even longer. StayOnTask is a free app for Android phones that gives you a sound at random intervals to keep your attention where you intend it to be. You just need to supply the rewards. We have seen group members' rewards include things they rarely allow themselves, such as sunflower seeds, or a long, appreciative sip of coffee.

We've arrived at part 3, replacing flashing lights with guiding lights. For Tonya's husband, replacing flashing lights with guiding lights meant that he had to replace his phone, computer, and other classroom distractions with a paper planner, which he color-coded. This way, at the moment assignments were given, he could write them into his planner, noting their due dates, and highlight the assignments with their designated color. When he looked at his planner, the colors gave him a visual of his day, so he knew which classes he'd be attending and which textbooks and folders he needed to put into his locker at school (for when it was homework time later). Outside class time, he had alarms set to tell him when to start homework. When he sat down to work, he set a timer with an alarm to tell him when to stop. Remember the four S's. There are no starts without stops.

If you want to add guiding lights to your environment, notice what difference their addition makes. Remember guiding lights are the usually steady, gentler lights that say, "Here's where you *really* want your attention to be right now."

Work

The same action and regulation skills needed for school are needed at work. As we mentioned before, the flashing lights and guiding lights may also be the same at work as they are at school. For example, if you work on a computer, websites irrelevant to your work may draw your attention away just as they can at school.

FLASHING LIGHTS

At work, maybe you have to be on a computer. Then what? You may have to fight technology with technology. Yes, technology exists to keep us away from technology. In 2013, NPR ran an article describing the apps SelfControl and Freedom. With SelfControl, a free Mac application, you can block websites of your choosing for up to 24 hours (Baek 2013). No cheating allowed. If you change your mind and restart the computer or delete the app, the websites you blocked stay blocked for the number of hours you specified. Freedom blocks all Internet access. These or other "anti-distraction apps" may fit your needs.

You can also go low-tech when fighting technology. If your phone distracts you and you use it to be aware of the time and for alarms, get a watch (no smart watch, that's cheating).

Another common distraction at work happens to be other people. They may come by your work area to chat with you right when you need to focus on work (after all, you may be quite social and like talking). How do you let them know when it's the right time and when it's the wrong time to interrupt you? One way is by posting a sign. Here's where you can use your creativity. A colleague with ADHD puts a sign on her office door that says it's "crunch time" and she needs to "hunker down" and remain undisturbed. When this colleague's ready for company, she removes the sign (or just opens her door). Some people put "visiting hours" on their door.

Are we still missing your main distraction at work? If it's a wandering mind or emotions, such as anxiety, continue on to the guiding lights section below.

GUIDING LIGHTS

For work, we recommend both the same kinds of guides we discussed for school (such as planners) and something that you may have never heard of before (that you can apply to school, too): an entrance ritual and an exit ritual. These are guiding lights of the cueing variety. And, for some of you, background noise between the time of your entrance and exit rituals may work as a guiding light.

Guide 1: Rituals. Do you often seem to be a high-speed freight train when you get to work and when you leave? You come through without pausing at the train station that is your workplace, carrying mental cargo (such as anxiety or thoughts about the past or future) that fragments your focus? An entrance ritual is like stopping at the train station, first, to drop off cargo no longer needed for the next leg of your trip and, second, to map out this next leg.

One way to drop off your mental cargo is by pausing to create presence. Yes, pause. Then bring your mind to the present moment. This can involve as little as two minutes of closing your eyes and noticing your breath just as it is, without evaluating or trying to change it. Just notice it with openness and curiosity, and, when your mind wanders away from the breath, notice the wandering. Then bring your attention back. This is a mindfulness meditation practice. You may already be familiar with mindfulness. If not, know that the next chapter tells you more about mindfulness. If you are skeptical about the power of mindfulness, that's okay; we hope you'll just be open to trying it. For now, go ahead and put down the book and try noticing your breath as described.

After you drop off unneeded cargo, map out the next leg of your trip: your workday. This means planning your workday rather than rushing forward without a clear vision. The minutes you give to planning up front can save you many more lost minutes later. Just as for school, this means having a planner to note what you need to do when, and to prioritize tasks. See our resource section at the end of the book for resources to learn *how* to prioritize, if needed, and an app that may help with this, if desired.

There are no entrances without exits and no exits without entrances. You need an exit ritual to accompany your entrance ritual. Just like an entrance ritual, an exit ritual helps you shift—another of the four S's—your attention to where you want it to be when you leave work (such as on family and friends). Also, paying attention to your ending point helps you with your next starting point.

The exit ritual mirrors the entrance one. First, go to your planner and note what you've accomplished and what needs to be moved to the next workday. Second, leave work cargo at the station of work before the next leg of your trip (away from work and to home, the gym, or whatever your next destination). To do this, again, pause and center yourself, such as through the mindfulness of your breath practice we described above.

(Potential) Guide 2: Background noise. We want to give you a potential guiding light at work to try along with your entrance and exit rituals. We call it a "potential" guiding light because research suggests that it increases focus for some and decreases focus for others. What is it? Background noise. Many whose attention wanders report that having background noise reduces "noise" inside their heads, allowing more focus. And research suggests that, indeed, this is the case, for some of you. It depends on the background noise. You might find a particular study on this interesting. In 2011, Pelham and colleagues tested the effect of background noise (specifically, music) on classroom behavior and performance of boys with and without ADHD. They found that for most of the boys (with and without ADHD) the music made no difference for their behavior and performance. For a subset of the boys with ADHD, however, music during class time helped and for a different subset of the boys with ADHD, music hurt. This same study, by the way, looked at the effect of playing videos of movies on boys' classroom behavior and performance and found that videos distracted both groups of boys but especially distracted the boys with ADHD. What's the message, then? First, stay away from background noise with visuals, such as leaving on a TV while you work. Second, experiment with audio background noise.

When you experiment with background noise, know that, for now, research indicates that music may be the safest way to go (per the Pelham study and other studies). Noise with words may be particularly distracting. So if you listen to talk radio while working, consider trying classical music instead. (If you do this, you will be experimenting with replacing flashing lights with guiding lights.)

Home

We've arrived at your home. With examples from two environments (school and work) presented already, we will focus on one of the most common flashing lights at home that we hear about, apart from other electronics: television.

FLASHING LIGHTS

If you have a television, there are many reasons to "kill your television," to borrow a phrase from John Medina; however, we will just stay focused on whether it's a distraction for you at home. That is, does it pull your attention from where you need it to be? If you think it's just background noise that increases your focus, consider that you may be wrong. One way to test this is to experiment with having the TV off. Experiment with a different background noise while you do the things that TV keeps you from doing.

If TV is indeed one of your flashing lights and you are, nonetheless, unwilling to part with it for good, what about making it harder to turn on? You could move the TV to a different location or lock up the remote, for example. This gives you time to notice the impulse to turn on the TV and to allow the impulse to pass, as all nonessential impulses will if you let them. If you obey the impulse, you still may find that the decreased ease of turning on the TV decreases how often it's on.

GUIDING LIGHTS

Now what about a guiding light at home? Here's a possibly novel one for you: a family meeting. Other people can be guiding lights as well as flashing ones. It depends on the circumstances and who's involved.

Guide 1: Rituals. We discussed entrance and exit rituals at work. Having these rituals at home can also direct your attention and action away, and prepare them for a change of context. Often we get home with work on our mind or leave home mentally carrying the chores of the day. An entrance ritual, where you orient yourself to being back at home through an intentional, meaningful practice, such as first greeting your family, pet, or plant (depending on your circumstances) and changing into home clothes or pausing to be mindful of your breath or body sensations, can help your mind shift to a change of scene. Similarly, an exit ritual of saying goodbye and pausing to notice an inhalation and exhalation as you step out the door can ease a shift of your attention and intention from one place to another.

Guide 2: Family meetings. Weekly to daily family meetings at home are rituals that let you, as a family, map out the what, who, and when of family life. What does everyone want to happen during the week? Who will do it? When will it happen? Sometimes how and where become relevant, too. And documentation's essential. Your family, whether it's a pair or a tribe, has to have the family meeting results documented and located somewhere for all to consult. This can mean a whiteboard on the fridge where each one's "duties" can be seen and crossed off as accomplished.

You could achieve your desired redesign of your environment with just this exercise of replacing flashing lights with guiding ones. This replacement is about giving you what Barkley (2012) calls "external real-time accommodations at key points of activity" while the activity is placed within its "natural settings." Said simply, it means having guiding lights for a particular activity at the very moment and place that you are working on the activity. Think about learning to swim. If you learn swim strokes and water safety only when you are away from water, you are unlikely to learn to swim. The right time and place to learn to swim is when you get into the water. In this case, you need a swim coach (external accommodation) who instructs you at the very moment (real-time) that you are moving your arms and legs (key points of activity) through water (the natural setting for swimming). If you get swim instruction only when you are *out of* the water, then you are unlikely to remember what to do when you actually *get into* the water. Barkley argues that because your brain's lacking internal sources to regulate your behavior, you require external ones. He calls it *externalizing* sources of motivation, drive, and memory. Guiding lights are external sources of memory and motivation. For a list of examples of these for use at school, work, and home, see appendix C. There's also a version online at http://www.newharbinger.com/34459 that we kept to one page so that you can print and post it.

If you're ambitious and want to continue to the second half of your redesign, continue reading.

Redesigning Environments for Your Future Self

Let's go back to what you are trying to accomplish with changing your environment(s). It is this: using what's known about your brain to match your exterior with your interior. We've talked about replacing your environment's flashing lights with guiding lights to match the needs of your interior attention.

There's something else that you can get when you have guiding lights at the right time and place: immediate reward. In the swimming example, what's your immediate reward? You swim instead of sink. And guess what? We all are swayed more by immediate rewards compared with ones we have to wait a long time for. But most of us can, if needed, put off immediate rewards for the sake of a bigger, future reward, unless… Yes, unless you have ADHD and understand this about your brain: Your brain has a *now* bias (Jackson and MacKillop 2016). Remember bias number 1? It's your bias toward the exciting over the boring. Your *now* bias is bias number 2. You are biased toward what you want now over what you want later. Because of this bias, your future self loses out to your present self. Have you ever noticed this when it comes to, say, starting or finishing a project at work, a writing assignment at school, or organization at home? Our group members often say that they intended to start or finish something and then an opportunity for something more fun or interesting presented itself. How can you make today matter for a graduation, promotion, or retirement that you want to celebrate months or years from now? How can you remember the difference a missed deadline today and tomorrow makes for your future self (and wealth)? We're glad you asked.

We use the acronym IRTT, which stands for "Introduce Results of Tomorrow Today." Your brain needs to register the results of tomorrow as today, to bring the future into the present. If you have your eye on a distant prize (health and wealth), a future one, the apparent distance from now to the prize weakens the power of the prize to motivate you. In the competition for your attention and action, tomorrow often loses to today.

How can you strengthen tomorrow's ability to compete with today? Have agents of tomorrow inhabit the present. Intrigued? Read below for examples of this. We start with an unpleasant agent (a stick) and then describe a pleasant one (a carrot). Threats and rewards both get your brain's attention.

This true story of bringing an agent of the future to the present comes from NPR's *Radiolab* podcast:

> *Zelda had smoked cigarettes for decades and tried to quit repeatedly without success…until she made a pact with a close friend. Zelda and her friend agreed that as soon as Zelda smoked, she'd have to tell her friend and give $5,000 to the KKK. Thereafter, every time Zelda had the urge to pick up a cigarette, she envisioned the KKK and having to send them money. Knowing that as soon as she acted on her urge, she'd have to send the KKK money greatly distressed her. She quit for good. Where the distant result of health and longevity failed (tomorrow's reward of quitting), the immediate result of funding a group she despised succeeded (NPR 2011).*

Zelda combined a compelling stick strategy called precommitment, in which she limited her choices before facing them. She did this by recruiting a friend to keep her accountable. If you have no one you can identify for this kind of accountabilty, help's available. One place for this help is http://www .StickK.com, which allows you to stay accountable just as Zelda was accountable to her friend and commit ahead of time to losing money (as Zelda did) if you give up on your goal. Maybe this scares you? You can choose the accountability part without the monetary loss, if you'd like. If the accountability turns out to be insufficient, you can later add the loss (which StickK sends to a charity of your choice—or an anti-charity, as the case may be). StickK may be what you need. It combines specific deadlines with accountability, both of which bring the future into the present. Tonya's seen it work for members of her groups who kept putting off working on goals, such as achieving a healthy weight by exercising at the gym three times a week.

If you have no one to keep you accountable and you prefer to stay away from websites, another example of precommitment would be to eliminate your choices before the point of decision—what some call "burning your ships" and Tonya calls "binding yourself." It's about truly eliminating your choices before they arrive. It can be helpful to try a visual. Hold both your fists out ahead of you. Now imagine that your right hand is the choice you want to make when faced with a decision, let's say to exercise. Your left hand is the other choice, the one to which you want to say no, let's say to skip exercise. Imagine your fists as how much time there is between you and when you will face the decision between these. What does "binding yourself" look like? Put your left hand behind your back. Imagine you've tied it there. You now have only the right fist out. You have eliminated your freedom to choose, knowing that this freedom to choose will lead to the wrong choice for you.

When she wanted to switch from driving to cycling, Tonya had to restrict her freedom to opt out. As long as she had her car available, it won out over her bike almost every morning before work, despite her weekend intentions to start and end her week with cycling. So she sold her car and her bike became a best friend. She also found this kind of precommitment helpful when it came to money. Usually, she spent about $7 a day at the café at the clinic where she worked on Tuesdays. One particular Tuesday, when her first coffee break of the day came, she desperately wanted to get her usual coffee. But she

53

had no money. She'd left it at home. So she had to learn how to use the coffeemaker at work and let go of the idea of needing a "special" coffee drink. And she saved $7. Now, if Tonya had had her money on her, she would have spent it, she has no doubt, despite the fact that she needed to save money for a family vacation. She would have put up a weak resistance. And that's the point of binding yourself: to remove your struggle before you face it. This works better than telling yourself that you will conquer your struggle at the moment it shows up, despite evidence to the contrary.

Money also happens to be an example of a pleasant agent of tomorrow. Yes, money works both ways. We work hard to keep from losing it and we work hard to get it. Research indicates, for example, that you'll exercise more when you get a little money for it. Small, immediate rewards work to keep you on the path to the tomorrow you want. You just need to be sure you know which rewards work for you and give them to yourself at the right time. The right time is right after you act to achieve your goal. In his 2011 Ted Talk, behavioral economist Dan Ariely calls using immediate rewards to motivate behavior you need to do *now* to obtain big future rewards "reward substitution." Let's look at an example of this.

If your goal is to save money for a vacation six months from now, each time you deposit money into an account for this, you can reward yourself with something that costs nothing. You could have a hot bath, give yourself a little vacation by going to a fancy hotel lobby and reading a magazine as if you're a guest (credit for this idea goes to Marsha Linehan), or call a friend for a guilt-free chat. Got your journal?

Experiment with rewarding yourself. Start by writing out a list of things that give you pleasure. Be sure your list includes things that are easily accessible to you and some things that require no money. Examples include sunflower seeds, a hot bath, reading a magazine for fun, going for a walk, a special home-brewed coffee drink, and so on.

Now it's your turn to put your exercises of Flashing Lights and Introduce Results of Tomorrow Today together. Yes, together, we are talking FLIRTT. (Remember, you are trying to attract your attention.) Below, see an example journal entry of FLIRTT and a numbered how-to.

CHALLENGE THYSELF 2: FLIRTT (FL+IRTT)

Here, we walk you through, step by step, how to work with both your biases—bias toward the exciting and bias toward the immediate—by combining the replacement of your flashing lights with a present-day agent of the future.

Part I. *Flashing Lights*

1. Pick an environment (e.g., school, work, home).

2. For this environment, identify your flashing lights (you can recruit someone to help).

3. For this environment, identify your guiding lights.

4. Replace your flashing lights with your guiding lights.

Example:

1. Environment: Home

2. Flashing Lights: Family members' activities and interruptions and dog

3. Guiding Lights: Assignment list, desk, white noise

4. Replacement:

    • Move to room with desk and assignment list

    • Wear headphones playing wordless music (close door)

Part II. *Introduce Results of Tomorrow Today*

1. Pick a stick or a carrot. Will you be more motivated by loss aversion? Pick a stick. What is it? Or will you be more motivated by reward? Go with a carrot. What is it? Remember to look at your list of rewards.

2. Now, as you achieve what you seek, whether it's saving money, starting and finishing school or work assignments, or completing tasks at home, either reward yourself or hold onto what you'd hate to lose (by avoiding the stick).

3. If needed, turn up the heat with high-level precommitment.

Example:

1. Carrot: For each assignment finished, reward will be 15 minutes of a favorite show.

2. Stick: For each assignment missed, stick will be giving away $15.

3. Precommitment: Recruit a reliable accountability buddy.

Feel free to reread this chapter before you move onto the next one, and work on these exercises until you have tried them several times. They are quite involved, really. Knowing your biases and how to influence them will be to your advantage when you read the next chapter. Getting to know your biases through the exercises will also be to your advantage if you forgo modifying your existing environments and, instead, exchange them for ones already designed just for you. Or you may combine modification and exchange.

Exchanging Environments

While writing this chapter, Tonya almost left this section out and it was during or on the edge of sleep that she realized her omission. During a car ride she had been discussing this chapter of this book with her husband and older child, both diagnosed with ADHD. Her older child spoke up and said, "A room full of puppies and candies." Tonya asked what this meant, and her child said it's what a room seems like to him. When asked what an *empty* room seems like, he described how he will notice the shapes, curves, and corners of the walls; bumps on the ceiling; light seeping under the door; and the texture of the floor, adding that carpet is like a maze of threads. He concluded, "Even an empty room is filled with so much. It's insane."

When everything's a distraction, there are two things you can do. First, you can dopaminize your guiding lights so that they are far more interesting than the flashing lights you are unable to banish from a room. Tonya's child has the immediate gratification of the point system that her family uses. Regulating his attention and his actions gets him points that can add up over the course of less than a week to an appealing reward of his choice. These points usually win out over the carpet threads. What small, immediate reward could win out over distractions that you are unable to banish? It can be points to a large reward or quarters toward a ten- or twenty-dollar purchase, depending on what works for you. There's something else you can do when everything distracts you: exchange environments. Exchange an environment that works against you for one that works for you. For Tonya's child, exchanging environments meant leaving a traditional school for one with a large emphasis on physical play, experiential learning, and creativity. Her son's school environment gives his stimulation-seeking brain various kinds of stimulation, all designed to educate. Tonya no longer gets e-mails from teachers, aware of his ADHD diagnosis, about how her son just has to work harder and put more effort into the whole enterprise or about how the teachers are "confused by" her son's forgetting lessons and assignments when they have told him what they were. Sound familiar? Many environments will ask you to change and may keep you so busy just trying to keep from drowning that you are unable to see that the pool across the way is neither too big nor too small but just right. Now what Tonya hears about her son is that he has "an unbridled enthusiasm for life" that keeps him highly engaged at school. Meanwhile, her son says that for the first time, he's able to keep up with his homework and he likes this. What a difference a change of environment makes.

Finding or carving out a niche for your attention and action biases may be what you need, at least until more work and school environments catch up with the brain research. Hartmann's hunter-farmer metaphor of ADHD, a favorite of Greg's, illustrates the point of finding one's niche.

Hunter-Farmer Metaphor

When his son was diagnosed with ADHD, Thom Hartmann told his son the following story. Once upon a time, we were divided into hunters and farmers. Both had their unique place, and each had their value. Hunters moved wide and far and fast, acting as predators for their groups. They had to develop broad, fast-moving attention; quickness to action; and the ability to hyper-focus on life-and-death moments to kill their prey and to survive. In contrast, farmers stayed close to home and crops, acting as gatherers for their groups. They had to develop relatively narrow, steady attention; the ability to stick with repetitive, prolonged actions; and be motivated by the more distant fruits of their labor. Hartmann describes your attention, as a person with ADHD, as a hunter's and your dilemma as being a hunter surrounded by a farmer-rewarding environment. Who better, farmer or hunter, to sit still listening to meetings or lectures and organizing paperwork?

Though Hartmann's metaphor is just a metaphor, or story, there's some evidence for its ideas. For example, a group of anthropologists and a biologist studied a tribe of Kenyans who formed two groups: nomads and those who had settled and stopped roaming (Eisenberg et al. 2008). In both groups, about 20% of members had a genetic mutation (*DRD4* genotype) associated with ADHD. Eisenberg and his colleagues found that the nomads with the gene mutation were better nourished than nomads without it *and* that the settlers with the gene mutation were less fit than settlers without it. They suggested that ADHD-like traits and related behaviors might be better suited to the dynamic and less predictable environment of a nomad than to settlers' life of agriculture and markets. Psychologist Rick Hanson (2015) even suggests that we as a species started off with hunter (or nomad) brains: "In order to survive, our ancestors evolved to be stimulation-hungry and easily distracted, continually scanning their interior and their environment for opportunities and threats, carrots and sticks" (1). Sound like someone you know?

"Finding Your Niche"

Using the hunter-farmer metaphor, finding your niche means choosing or creating environments or situations that reward your hunter brain and permit mutually rewarding hunter-farmer relationships. This book came into being because Greg did this. Greg, diagnosed with ADHD long ago, shares your low attention and action regulation. He also has dyslexia. Give him an audience, whether of one or 100, and he can capture his own and others' attention, telling stories that move, inspire, and educate others. He gives presentations all over the country to packed audiences, with glowing reviews. Speaking to audiences is a high-interest activity for Greg.

Ask Greg to write or type, and his words cease to flow. His brain seems to shut down. If you observed him sitting down to write, there's a good chance you'd see Greg's face form a pained expression as his pen hovered over paper. Several minutes later, he'd emit a frustrated sigh and jot down three words, notes on a thought. From these experiences, Greg's learned to rely heavily on his oral skills and to collaborate with others on writing projects.

When the opportunity for this book arose, Greg recruited Tonya as listener, collaborator, and writer. So talking to Tonya let Greg draw on his high-interest activity of speaking and navigate his low-interest, and tiring, activity of writing. At work, too, Greg maneuvered to play to his strengths. He sought a job as the head of mental therapy groups at Kaiser Permanente Northwest. There, he ran groups and guided other mental health therapists, which let him rely heavily on talking and his highly developed social skills. Whatever the context, Greg swims with his own tide and skillfully connects with others to find ways to get where he wants when the tides change. Even at home, he and his wife distribute chores and necessary tasks according to their interests and talents.

Before you leave this chapter, consider how you could choose and create environments and situations that reward your brain's wiring and that invite other-wired brains to collaborate.

Key Points from Chapter 2

- Your brain has two major biases: a bias toward what you find interesting or exciting and a *now* bias, a bias toward immediate gratification. Immediate gratification = dopamine!

- Research shows that relying on your brain to "just" remember these biases at the right time and then resist them when they work against you is ineffective. You need to redesign your environment so that your biases work for you.

- You need to identify flashing lights that pull your attention and action away from, and identify guiding lights that direct your attention and action to, where you need them. You need to work with both kinds of lights.

Removing or dimming your flashing lights lets you *stop* your attention and action from being a runaway train and to *shift* it to the track that leads to your desired destination. Your guiding lights show you where that track is, how to *start* on this track, and how to *sustain* your attention and action there.

- To guide your attention and action, you can alter your environment. Some environments compete too much for your attention and you lose to them. Other environments offer weak competition for your attention and you can focus on the prize. But to do this, you may need to add practical reminders of the prize to your environment.

- Through *Know Thyself 2,* you've identified:

  • the elements of your environment that pull your attention off the path where you want to be (distractions, like bright billboards or the wolf of *Little Red Riding Hood*), and

  • elements that keep you on the path (guides, like a lighthouse or compass).

- You can experiment, through *Challenge Thyself 2,* with replacing distractions with guides and introducing carrots or sticks, depending on what works for you, to keep your eye on the prize when the prize is a distant one. You can also practice restricting the freedom of your present self for the sake of your future self through precommitment, or "burning your ships."

- Consider ways that you can exchange environments that ask you to sit still, be quiet, focus on the future, and do the same thing repeatedly for a long time with ones that fit your brain's biases.

CHAPTER 3

Healthy Habits for Attention and Action Regulation

You know from years of news articles and public service announcements about healthy habits. And you know from what we've told you that healthy habits help your attention and action regulation. But do you know that your health habits are altering your experiences and genes? Grant you, we've known about our ability to change our experiences through our behavior for quite a while. This is straight-up psychology. But it's only been since the mid-1990s that scientists have confirmed that we can influence our *genes* through our experiences, both active (what we do) and passive (what happens to us). Welcome to the world of epigenetics—gene control by factors other than your DNA sequence—where environments and behaviors can switch genes on and off and determine which cellular proteins are decoded (Simmons 2008). In this chapter, we focus on behaviors and habits that change you several layers deep, all the way to the expression of genes that influence attention and action.

The Foundation of Physical and Mental Health

We like to build on strong foundations. It just makes sense. If you try to build on a weak foundation, all that you've built will easily fall apart. As our brains and bodies would have it, the same three factors form the foundation of both physical and mental health: sleep, nutrition, and exercise. These factors bear on specific areas of functioning, such as your attention and action regulation, overall functioning, and biological and epigenetic aging (see Tsubota 2015).

ADHD and Healthy Living: When and Where to Intervene

In 2016, researchers examined whether children seven to eleven years old with ADHD have a similar number of healthy lifestyle behaviors (including sleep, nutrition, and physical activity) when compared with typically developing children from the same community (Holton & Nigg 2016).

They found that even after adjusting for age, sex, IQ, household income, four comorbid psychiatric disorders, and ADHD medication use, children with ADHD were nearly twice as likely to have fewer healthy behaviors. This means that with these other factors equal, ADHD increases the probability of fewer healthy lifestyle behaviors.

Perhaps related to these behaviors and showing their cost, another recent study that followed hundreds of children with and without ADHD born from 1976 to 1982 to adulthood found that the girls with ADHD were twice as likely to be obese adults compared with girls without ADHD (Aguirre Castaneda et al. 2016).

In sum, the research suggests that low attention and action regulation coexists with a higher chance of a weaker foundation of health as early as elementary-school age. Anyone for keeping recess at, and junk food out of, school?

If you think you've heard everything about sleep, exercise, and nutrition, we want you to know two things: (1) what becomes "common knowledge" is often mistaken and (2) we share the latest research with you as of the time of this writing.

Sleep

Do you know what regular sleep deprivation looks like? It looks like low attention and action regulation. The same symptoms of forgetfulness, distractibility, disorganization, and careless mistakes that reveal low attention and action regulation show up when any of us are sleep deprived. Sleep matters so much to our ability to pay attention that an essential part of diagnosing ADHD is ruling out whether your symptoms—losing things, distractibility, forgetfulness, careless mistakes—come from sleep deprivation or disturbances (e.g., Thakkar 2013; Hvolby 2015; Fischman, Kuffler, & Bloch 2015). This is tricky. It's tricky because, if you are chronically sleep deprived, your low attention and action regulation may be the result of both chronic sleep deprivation and ADHD. In some cases, it may even be the result of chronic sleep deprivation *instead of* ADHD (Fischman et al. 2015), which is why careful diagnosis requires knowing your sleep. But, as we said, it's tricky, because the relationship between ADHD and sleep can be so darn complicated.

ADHD appears to increase the chance of having a diagnosable sleep disorder, such as obstructive sleep apnea (e.g., Hvolby 2015). And even without such a sleep disorder, sleep disturbances, namely decreased sleep duration and quality, are common to ADHD. Recent research suggests that the sleep woes of those with ADHD may be caused by disturbed circadian rhythms and points to a future where intervention targets the circadian clock to relieve symptoms of ADHD (Coogan, Baird, Popa-Wagner, & Thome 2016). Until this happens, we know that for many with ADHD, it can be hard to get to sleep (Brown 2008). Yet you may have to get up early, creating a cycle of late to bed, early to rise and of chronic sleep deprivation, which has consequences down to your genes. Even *one* all-nighter can alter biological clock genes (Cedernaes et al. 2015).

Regardless of complicating factors, throw some sleep deprivation at our brains, and they have even less energy for attention and action regulation. This is true even for people with high attention and action regulation. Sleep deprivation depletes us all. But because you have ADHD, the result for you is extremely low attention and action regulation. It's why mastering your attention and action starts with sleep. If there's only one thing you do to increase your control of your attention and action, you want it to be getting enough sleep. And even if you have a sleep disorder, a big part of your sleep equation is your sleep environment and sleep behavior (both of which influence your brain activity relevant to sleep). We can help. (As Tonya's husband, Sergio, comments, "Yeah, Tonya will put you to sleep at 8 p.m." He's leaving out that Tonya gets up at 5 a.m.)

Fascinating Link Between Sleep and Exercise

It may be common knowledge that exercise during the day helps us sleep at night, but it turns out that exercise may also undo abnormalities to our gene expression resulting from any severe disruptions to our mothers' sleep while pregnant with us.

Consider this...

Researchers found that mice who had early-life physical activity showed a reversal of negative epigenetic changes caused by researchers' disrupting the sleep of their mothers while they were pregnant with them (Mutskov et al. 2015).

Sleep and Attention

You probably know that healthy sleep starts with getting enough of it (hence Tonya's schedule). And you may know that, if you get enough uninterrupted sleep time, you're likely to enter all its glorious stages. But—and we warned you—what you think you know about how much sleep you need may change if you continue reading. We want to set the record straight about the number of hours of recommended sleep for adults.

You may have heard that we need about seven hours. Here's the truth: seven hours is the *minimum* recommended number of hours for adults. The National Sleep Foundation (2015) relied on 18 leading sleep scientists and researchers examining the most rigorous sleep studies to come up with these recommendations as of 2015: seven to nine hours of sleep for adults under age 65 and seven to eight hours for adults aged 65 and older. Yet many hold the *minimum* recommended number as the *recommended* number. This raises the question of why. If our corporate culture's fears of reduced "productivity" contribute to this bias toward less sleep, the irony is that getting enough sleep enhances mental and physical speed and sharpness (Goel et al. 2009). The National Sleep Foundation's recommendations, after all, reflect what research as a whole shows to be the amount of sleep associated with optimal physical and mental fitness.

When it comes specifically to paying attention, research suggests that eight hours trump seven. In 2003, two prominent studies came out answering the question of how sleep affects our ability to sustain attention and other cognitive functions. One of these studies, out of the University of Pennsylvania, restricted individuals' sleep for two weeks, longer than any study before it (Van Dongen et al. 2003). And no one could cheat because all participants lived at the research lab for the entire two weeks as researchers objectively measured their sleep and kept them from nodding off. Researchers placed participants into one of three sleep groups: four, six, or eight hours of sleep each night. Each day, every two hours, researchers measured participants' ability to sustain attention while performing a tedious task and measured their working memory. Both abilities are relevant to you because decreased ability to sustain attention to tedious tasks and decreased working memory characterize ADHD.

The other prominent study on sleep and attention occurred at the Walter Reed Army Institute of Research, where participants were sent to bed for no more than three, five, seven, or nine hours each day for one week (Belenky et al. 2003). Here, too, researchers monitored participants at the lab, so no one could sleep more than allowed. The researchers measured these participants' ability to sustain attention to the same tedious task that the other study used.

Both studies showed that at less than eight hours of sleep, our ability to sustain attention suffers, day after day. For all groups getting less than eight hours, participants' ability to sustain attention declined *every* day of the study with one exception. The seven-hour group's attention declined every day for three days and then stayed at this lower, three-day level for the rest of the study. Actually, even after the sleep-deprivation period ended and participants received three eight-hour nights of sleep, the seven-hour group members' ability to sustain their attention stayed at this lower level. (The researchers stopped the study after this three-day post-deprivation period, so they left us all with the cliff-hanger of how many more days the subjects' impaired attention lasted.)

The first study also looked at working memory, one of the brain functions that ADHD affects. (You know it as difficulty remembering where you just put something, what someone just said, and what you were about to say; and difficulty holding onto an idea while paying attention to other tasks.) The researchers found that at six or fewer hours of sleep, participants' working memory suffered.

There's one more finding we want to share. Participants sleeping six and four hours each day for two weeks insisted that their lack of sleep had no effect on their performance. In fact, by the end of the study, they were performing at the level of someone legally drunk. Apparently, as when drunk, when sleep deprived, we're poor judges of our performance ability.

YOUR SLEEP

If you get less than eight hours of sleep, and you're willing to be both researcher and participant, here's *Know Thyself 3 for Sleep*. It outlines recommendations from the Division of Sleep Medicine at Harvard Medical School (2008).

KNOW THYSELF 3 FOR SLEEP: How Much Sleep Do You Need?

Choose any or all of the following three ways you can evaluate your sleep needs.

Notice your levels of alertness and sleepiness during the day. For even just three days, pay attention to when you feel most alert during the day and when you feel fatigue descending on you. You'll likely be most accurate if you have your journal or planner handy to write down when during the day you feel most alert and when the most tired. Be sure to notice when you have woken up after falling asleep during the day, such as during a meeting, at your desk, or on the bus to work. You may see these as normal naps when they may be telling you that you need more sleep. It is normal, John Medina (2014) points out, to want to nap about 12 hours from the halfway point of your sleep (so if you sleep from 10 p.m. to 6 a.m., 2 a.m. would be your halfway point and 2 p.m. would be when your brain would want to nap). He also points out that it may be advantageous to nap briefly (about 20 to 30 minutes) at this time.

Track your sleep using a sleep diary. Turn parts of your journal into a sleep diary or download one (see appendix A: Resources). Your sleep diary is a grid that can vary from basic to comprehensive. A comprehensive one may show each day of the week and, for each day, how many minutes you nap altogether, what time you go to bed, how many minutes until you fall asleep, how many hours you sleep, the number of awakenings you have, how long the awakenings last altogether, how alert you feel the next day (1–10 scale, 10 = most alert), final wake time, and time out of bed. The National Sleep Foundation has a comprehensive sleep diary. If this seems to be too much, you can just track what time you go to sleep and what time you wake up daily, creating a visual of this by shading boxes. For example, the first part of it could look like the example below. You'd want to add columns for all 24 hours of the day instead of the "..." we have below. And it's helpful to add an "A" into a box for alcohol use, a "C" for caffeine, and an "E" for exercise. In the example below, notice that 6 a.m. and 7 a.m. are shaded. The shading offers a visual of the morning hours slept this particular day. Shading each day for a week reveals patterns. Tonya uses this kind of grid with her ADHD groups and often hears members' surprise at what they uncover. They sometimes find that their occasional nightcap occurs daily, their little bit of inconsistency is a lot of inconsistency, or their pet interrupts their sleep more often than they thought.

Day/ Date	Notes	6 a.m.	7a.m.	8 a.m.	...	Hours Slept
Mon/ 16th	Out of town Sat & Sun			C		8.5
Tues/ 17th						

Track your sleep for one week, completing the chart each morning after the previous night's sleep. Give yourself no more than 30 seconds to fill it out. No need to overthink it. A sleep diary can require less than five minutes' time over the course of an entire week. And just by tracking your sleep, you may begin to change it.

Give yourself a sleep vacation. Intrigued? If you have about two weeks of flexible time, consider a sleep vacation. Here's how it works. First, pick and stick to a bedtime so that you go to bed at the same time each night. Second, allow your body to wake up naturally, without an alarm clock. After about two weeks, if you're consistent, you'll start sleeping about the same number of hours, likely between seven and nine, each day. This will be how much sleep you need.

If you need to increase your sleep, we're here for you. The thing is, you need others to be here for you, too. One of the biggest challenges you may face to protecting your sleep time is getting others onboard. If this is the case, we have some suggestions.

CHALLENGE THYSELF 3 FOR SLEEP: How to Get the Sleep You Need

Prioritize sleep time and protect it. To get needed sleep, you first have to prioritize it. Getting to bed on time has to matter to you for it to matter to others. And once you prioritize your sleep, you need to protect it. You need to protect it even when others pooh-pooh your need for sleep or try to convince you that "you'll be fine." Stay firm and others will come to see that you mean it. Let them know that what they get is your ability to pay more attention to them when you're awake.

Develop a sleep ritual. A sleep ritual will cue your body that it's time to sleep. Our bodies and brains rely on sleep cues. Child care centers cue babies and toddlers by dimming the lights and putting on soothing music or sounds when it's nap time. You too can cue yourself for sleep by dimming the lights, turning off the screens, and practicing a calming ritual before bed, perhaps a mindfulness meditation or a breathing technique such as paced breathing or belly breathing (see our resource section, if needed).

Both paced and belly breathing put on the brakes of your body. To do paced breathing, make your exhalations longer than your inhalations. You can count the length of your exhalations and inhalations inside your head or by using the second hand of a watch. If you prefer, you can also try a paced breathing app. To do belly breathing, place a hand on your chest and the other on your belly and, as you breathe, notice the rise and fall of your chest compared with your belly. Try this now, moving your breath from your chest to belly to raise your belly when you inhale and sink your belly when you exhale. To see how many inhalation-exhalation cycles you need to calm your body, find your pulse at your wrist or neck and count your heartbeat for ten seconds. Write down how many times your heart beats for these ten seconds. Then do paced or belly breathing for a minute (time it) and check your pulse again for ten seconds. Did it lower? Unless your heart rate was already low when you began, increase the time you practice the breathing technique by one minute until you notice a reduction. And leave this exercise alone if you already consistently have low pulse (no need to get you fainting!).

Consult your doctor. Please consult with a doctor or nurse practitioner about your sleep if you find that on most days your eyelids feel heavy when you want to be awake, however many hours you sleep. Remember, diagnoses of ADHD and sleep disorders often come in pairs. Scientists are still trying to sort out why. You can also ask your medical practitioner about changing sleep-disrupting habits through cognitive behavioral therapy for insomnia (CBT-I), which is approved by the American Academy of Sleep Medicine as an effective therapy for insomnia.

You may want to try the sleep exercises alone for a few weeks before you move on to the next section. Getting enough sleep will actually help you with the other two parts of your foundation.

Nutrition

More and more, science tells us that what, and how much we eat can prevent and protect against diseases on the one hand and propagate them on the other. Few among us deny a connection between nutrition and type 2 diabetes, for example. But when it comes to specific nutrients to eat for our health, particularly brain health, contradictions and complications arise. It's hard—one nutrient interacts with so many others. We spare you these contradictions and complications and keep it simple, which means we stay away from what's popular and even positive—such as antioxidants—if there are several negative side effects and drug interactions to consider. This leaves us with three specific nutrients for you to consider for your brain health: omega-3s on the "yea" side, and trans and saturated fats on the "nay" side. We'll start with looking at how to get these on or off your plate, move to guidelines about what a healthy plate has, and then talk about the plate itself.

OMEGA-3S

Normal brain function, from fetal development on, depends on omega-3s. Neurons function poorly without them. Memory and learning suffer. This appears true for all of us. Of particular interest, omega-3 deficiency appears linked to ADHD and other psychiatric disorders. And the link is strong enough for some clinician-researchers to suggest that inpatient clinics begin routinely measuring psychiatric patients' blood fatty acid levels at the time of admission and offer supplementation as needed (Messamore & McNamara 2016).

Supplementation may help increase attention regulation. In 2011, Yale researchers reviewed studies on omega-3 fatty acid supplementation with children diagnosed with ADHD and found that supplementation reduced the children's symptoms (Bloch & Qawasmi 2011). The higher the dose, the higher the

73

reduction (750 mg was the highest dose given), whether the children were medicated or medication-free. A more recent review of omega-3 fatty acid effects on children's ADHD symptoms noted that supplementation showed "modest" but reliable effects on hyperactivity by parent and teacher report, and reliable effects for inattention by parent report (Hawkey & Nigg 2014). In this review, the researchers point out that it remains to be seen whether only those with below-normal blood levels of fatty acids benefit from supplementation. Larger effects of omega-3 fatty acids may appear if researchers focus on study participants who start off with low levels of fatty acids. Clearer effects may also appear if researchers look at the ratio of omega-3 and omega-6 fatty acids instead of looking at the levels of each separately (LaChance et al. 2016).

While researchers refine their answers regarding whom, what, and how much, there's enough evidence for you to try omega-3s for attention and action regulation, given their overall low risk, high accessibility, and various other health benefits—including, if research on worms applies to us, possibly increased longevity (Rangaraju et al. 2016). Omega-3 fatty acids are easy to get. Eat fish, especially oily ones that contain less mercury. A useful tip is to choose prey such as salmon and albacore tuna and avoid predators such as shark and swordfish. Fish oil also has few negative side effects beyond leaving a fishy smell at large quantities, unless you have a bleeding condition or are on medicines that can increase bleeding time if you become injured, such as anticoagulants ("blood thinners") or nonsteroidal anti-inflammatory drugs (NSAIDs). If increased risk of bleeding time applies to you, consult with your physician before upping your omega-3 levels. If no increased risk applies but you avoid fish, hemp oil also has high levels of omega-3 fatty acids. So does flax seed oil, but its high level of saturated fat dampens our enthusiasm for it.

TRANS AND SATURATED FATS

If omega-3s are the good guys, trans and saturated fats are the bad guys of brain health. Rodent studies show that they impair learning and brain functioning after only three weeks and that a saturated-fat diet negatively affects both the working memory performance and the hippocampus of middle-aged rats. (The hippocampus is our brain's main location for memory and learning.) In June 2015, given just how dastardly a villain trans fat is, the US government ordered manufacturers to stop using it within three years. But there's no need for you to wait three years or even another day.

You can reduce these villainous fats several ways. First, eat these things: fruits, vegetables, whole grains, nuts, fish, low-fat dairy, poultry, and naturally occurring, unhydrogenated vegetable oils (such as safflower, sunflower, or olive oil, especially virgin or extra virgin olive oil). Second, avoid these things: red meat, sugary foods and drinks, processed foods, deep-fried foods, and partially hydrogenated or hydrogenated vegetable oils. Fully hydrogenated oils are solid at room temperature (e.g., Crisco vegetable shortening). Partially hydrogenated oils include cottonseed, soybean, and peanut oils. If the potential dietary changes that face you seem overwhelming, pick only one or two changes to start. Because hydrogenated vegetable oil contributes 80% to 90% of the trans fats we eat (Pennsylvania State University 2006), and many of the major sources of these fats are also major sources of saturated fats, start with one change: avoiding fully or partially hydrogenated vegetable oils. This means avoiding sweet baked foods (pastries, cakes, pie crusts) and deep-fried foods (French fries, fried chicken, doughnuts). What a difference this can make! If you are ambitious, you can add fatty beef and lamb to the list of foods to avoid because of their saturated fats.

NUTRITION AND ATTENTION

Healthy eating helps your attention and action regulation, and also requires attention and action regulation. Part of attention and action regulation involves planning and managing time. Healthy eating requires planning what you are going to eat, how much, and when. A lack of planning seems to lead more often to unhealthy choices, such as fast food, than to healthy ones. It can also lead to non-hunger reasons for eating, such as boredom or stress. But thinking ahead is just one part of healthy eating. You also need guiding lights that attract your attention to healthy eating and you need to reduce flashing lights, such as a box of doughnuts out on the counter. Use cues as guiding lights for healthy eating. Look around your kitchen. What do you see? What food can you easily access? What reminders do you have to prepare a meal ahead of time, such as a lunch carrier? How much competition from flashing lights do your guiding ones have?

Research shows that many different cues influence our eating without our awareness. Brian Wansink, Director of the Cornell Food and Brand Lab at Cornell University, studies how cues affect our eating and has shown, along with his colleagues, that packaging size, portion size, the shape of a beer glass, language, and various external cues all contribute to our eating without our realizing it (Wansink 1996; Wansink & van Ittersum 2005). We often eat more than we think we do (and more than we need). How big are your plates and bowls at home? (Remember we said we'd talk about your plate.) Bigger cues you to eat more. If you'd like to know more about environmental cues, see Dr. Wansink's website, http://www.mindless eating.org.

Remember, too, your *now* bias, and use the power of pre-commitment to harness it. You may intend to eat healthy and find that the smells of the bakery on the way to your destination defeat your intention. Eliminate unhealthy food choices at home and work and consider changing your route to your destination to win the battles before they start.

Even when you plan ahead for healthy eating and its enemies, you have to have enough time to follow through with your plan. Time seems to be an obstacle to healthy eating for many Americans. Add low attention and action regulation to the mix, and creating enough time for healthy eating can seem like a major obstacle. Consider Josh's story.

> *Josh, because of his ADHD, never seemed to have enough time, especially for eating and almost never for cooking. Breakfast? Forget it. It was hard enough to get to work on time. Sometimes he'd stop for coffee and a pastry to eat while driving. When lunch came, he often discovered that, during the morning rush out the door, he'd forgotten his lunch (even when it was out on the kitchen counter). Anyway, he could always grab a granola bar at work (his employer kept them available for employees), which he sometimes ate at his desk. Sometimes he lost track of time at work and never made it to the granola bar. He always had dinner. Arriving home famished, he ate at a fast, furious pace, choosing whatever was quick and easy rather than healthy.*

Josh's story illustrates a few things that can come between you and healthy eating. Some may be more obvious, such as skipping breakfast or turning it into a pastry and coffee. Skipping breakfast tends to lead to less healthy food choices over the course of the day and, well, we think you know that a pastry qualifies as an unhealthy food choice. Some aspects of unhealthy eating may be less obvious. Tonya calls them speed eating and distracted eating. Because of your brain's craving for excitement and stimulation, you may be more prone to both. Both make it hard to notice what you really like and when your body says, "Stop! I'm full." Both can lead to overeating and unhealthy choices.

YOUR NUTRITION

We've given you a menu of healthy eating options: the omega-3 special, the trans- and saturated-fat-free platter, and a planning and time management combo. The paced-and-purposeful plate is coming up. If you came to this section of the book hungry for healthy eating and only read the menu, you would stay hungry. You need to eat to satisfy your hunger. Here's your chance. If you are uncertain what changes to focus on, start by learning more about your eating.

KNOW THYSELF 3 FOR NUTRITION: What Are You Eating?

For one week or two, use your journal to track your eating. Your tracking can have a column for each day of the week and five rows, to include any between-meal snacks. Create boxes big enough to jot down the time you eat and whether you're rushed, stressed, or multi-tasking while eating or simply highlight these times (with highlighting, circling, or some visual way to have these times pop out for you).

	Mon	Tues	Wed	Thurs	Fri	Sat	Sun
Breakfast							
Snack							
Lunch							
Snack							
Dinner							

When you've finished tracking your eating for a week or two, look back at what you ate when you were rushed, stressed, or multitasking. These are likely to be your go-to foods. We are going to learn more about them through mindful eating.

Mindful eating means noticing with curiosity what you eat, your response to it, and how you eat. It's the opposite of distracted speed eating (distracted eating and speed eating often go together). All by itself, it increases healthy eating choices and habits and for this reason has become part of the curriculum of eating disorder groups at many hospitals and clinics. We'll teach it to you so you can learn more about your go-to foods and then use mindful eating for foods of all kinds. As with all things truly mindful, it's both simple and hard to do. It's a skill that requires practice.

CHALLENGE THYSELF 3 FOR NUTRITION:
Mindful Eating

How much do you like your go-to food(s)? Do you even *really* like them? Does this liking, if it's there, stay with you bite after bite or does it change? Are you willing to test this? Before you get to your go-to food(s) or any foods you'd like to use for this exercise, clear your space of distractions and multitasking temptations (no reading, talking, checking messages, working, watching TV, or playing video games). Then, proceed, as follows:

1. Before you have a bite, use your senses to notice everything you can about the food you are about to eat. What does it look like? Is it one color or multiple? Which ones? What shape(s) do you see? What does it smell like? Does it have one smell or different ones (think of a wine or coffee connoisseur trying to detect scents)? Does it have a sound? If it's a kind of food you touch, what does it feel like? What are its textures?

2. Now put one bite into your mouth and notice the textures and tastes on your tongue, teeth, and elsewhere inside your mouth. What do you feel on your teeth as you chew? Swallow only after you've identified these things. If you are using utensils, put them down between bites.

3. As you eat, notice how hungry you are on a scale of one to ten and aim to stop when your body's had enough, left neither famished nor overfilled. Notice your level of satisfaction before you add another helping to your plate.

4. For a one-page mindful eating tip sheet that you can print and keep, see our resource section. Also, see http://www .mindlesseating.org for additional ideas on how to move from mindless to mindful eating as well as free visual cues.

As you work on healthy eating, remember to dopaminize it. If healthy eating matters to you but is a low-interest activity, turn up your interest. If you like being social, for example, try eating healthy meals with family or friends. To indulge creativity or competitiveness, hold some healthy cooking evenings where the available ingredients are all healthy ones. You can see what you can create on your own, cocreate with family members, or even see what different family members do with the same ingredients. You may have allowed yourself such fun when you were younger.

Exercise

John Medina (2014) wrote of twelve things that scientists know for sure about how our brains work. Of these only twelve "brain rules," it's fascinating to notice brain rule #1: "Exercise boosts brain power." It boosts exactly the kind of brain power you want: attention and action regulation.

Why might exercise matter so much for brain health? John Medina proposes that it's because our ancestors moved so much, walking about 12 miles a day. Our ancestors had to be able to pay attention while moving. Their survival depended on it. Ours no longer does but our brains have yet to show they've received the message. Physical activity increases our ability to focus. In fact, some argue that our corporate culture and our more sedentary lifestyles especially disadvantage the stimulus-seeking brains among us (this means you). Our culture may reward paying attention when bored and seated still (at meetings, at school) but our brains still reward getting physical.

The Exercised Brain Is a Replenished Brain

(Maddock et al. 2016)

Researchers at UC Davis found that vigorous exercise replenishes glutamate and GABA, two neurotransmitters often found depleted among adults diagnosed with major depressive disorder.

One way that exercise increases brain power is by increasing blood flow to the prefrontal cortex, the attention- and action-regulating part of our brains. Increase blood flow and you increase, as John Medina puts it, "mental sharpness" (2014). Another way that exercise increases brain power is by increasing the creation, survival, and resilience of neurons. We're talking neurogenesis and neuroplasticity. All that you need to remember is that your brain loves exercise. When you exercise, your brain releases various chemicals, including dopamine and endorphins, so you feel more motivated and happier at the same time.

Exercise and Epigenetics

(Denham et al. 2014)

We know that regular physical exercise increases longevity and spares us many chronic diseases, but how?

Enter epigenetic research which shows that exercise affects gene expression within cells throughout the body—brain, heart, bone, muscle, mouth, and fat—including *directly* altering fat formation.

EXERCISE AND ATTENTION

Your brain also shows you love when you exercise by increasing your attention. One session of aerobic exercise can noticeably increase focus, particularly under *unexciting* conditions. Researchers at the University of Illinois at Urbana–Champaign tested this out, using preadolescent children with and without ADHD (Pontifex et al. 2013). They gave these children unexciting tests of reading, math, and attention control at the start of the study and then, later, under two conditions. The two conditions were (1) after 20 minutes of moderate-intensity aerobic exercise and (2) after 20 minutes of seated reading. Half the children had condition 1 first and half had condition 2 first. The researchers measured children's performance and their brain activity during the tasks at the start of the study and after each condition. What do you think they found? With or without ADHD, children performed best on *all* the tasks after exercise. Exercise increased everyone's attention regulation, which fits with what we know about exercise. But there was more. The children with ADHD showed an "added benefit" of increased *action* regulation after exercising. Their brain activity showed increased "action monitoring processes," and they were better able to stay on task. Exercise may be just what you need before work meetings or class lectures.

We found only one study, out of the University of Georgia, that looked at the effects of exercise on adults with ADHD, and its methods looked very similar to the study on children described above. Adult men with ADHD both stayed seated for 20 minutes and exercised for 20 minutes, with half starting with sitting and half starting with exercise. After 20 minutes of moderately intense cycling, men reported increased motivation for mental tasks, feelings of energy, and reduced feelings of confusion, fatigue, and depression (Fritz & O'Connor 2016). They found no immediate effect on attention, however, as measured by reaction time and performance on a task requiring sustaining attention.

Although researchers have yet to give the effects of exercise on adult ADHD much attention, we know something about the relationship between exercise and ordinary adults' attention and action regulation. In Australia, for example, a psychologist and biologist teamed up to look at the effects of exercise on self-regulation of various forms (Oaten & Cheng 2006). They gave 24 adults from 18 to 50 years of age, none exercising regularly, a free gym membership and cheerleading to use it for two months. By the end of the study, these adults were hitting the gym three times a week on average. And their attention and action regulation blossomed. They showed increased ability to pay attention and to ignore distractions as objectively measured by task performance. On top of this, the participants reported reduced procrastination, smoking, drinking, impulsive buying, TV watching, and junk eating. They also reported saving more money, eating more healthy food, keeping up better with household chores, and arriving on time for appointments more often. Sign us up!

YOUR EXERCISE (VARY YOUR ROUTINE)

Okay, you say, exercise increases our fitness and health all the way to our genes, but you likely want to know how much exercise. Again, research indicates that even a single dose of 20 minutes of aerobic exercise rewards your brain and body. Ultimately, what the US Centers for Disease Control and Prevention (2015b) recommend is to aim for 150 minutes a week. If achieving 150 minutes a week seems insurmountable, focus on doing what you can. You could break the 150 minutes into 30 minutes five days a week or even into 10-minute doses. How about an energetic 10-minute walk outside during a lunch break? This would get you 50 minutes during the week and leave two 30-minute periods of exercise for the weekend.

Sometimes the word "exercise" conjures up images of sweat, tears, exhaustion, and even embarrassment. Sometimes it conjures up images of ecstasy. We want to encourage realistic thinking about exercise because we've seen how an all-or-nothing approach works out. An all-or-nothing approach can lead to avoidance or early abandonment. In one of his ADHD groups, Greg worked with somebody who planned to start exercising by running almost 30 miles, which he'd last run about 20 years prior. Greg calls this "I-must-run-a-marathon" thinking and advises switching to "I-will-run-for-one-minute-and-go-from-there" thinking. In her groups, Tonya has noticed that members who start "big" demonstrate what McGonigal (2013) calls the "what-the-hell" effect—they give up on what they start after a slip. "I scheduled exercise three days this week and missed my first day," they might say, "so, what the hell, I'll just miss it the whole week." This can then become, "I missed last week so, what the hell, I'll put it off one more week" until the entire plan's abandoned.

We advise against extremes. Instead, we suggest looking at what's realistic for you, including accommodating for any limitations due to medical conditions (consider consulting with a doctor, even if it's just by phone, about what's safe for you). To increase aerobic exercise, which is the kind associated with healthy brains, see below for ideas to start. Some exercise is better than no exercise. And exercise outdoors, if you can. Nature restores us and our ability to regulate our attention (Jaffe 2010), so combining exercise and nature promises the biggest results for your time.

KNOW THYSELF 3 FOR EXERCISE: What Aerobic Exercise Works for You?

Take out your journal and identify what aerobic exercise will work for you because a) you are willing to try it and b) you have access to this kind of exercise. For example, swimming will work if you are willing to swim and have access to a safe body of water. Consider walking, dancing, biking, running, playing sports, hiking, skiing, yoga, household chores, and yard work. Consider classes, using free online exercise videos (YouTube has many ten-minute ones), or getting exercise DVDs from the library. To be aerobic, the exercise will need to get your heart rate up (for a link to the USDA's physical activity guidelines, see our resource section).

Next identify where and when you'll exercise as well as how long. The point is to get real and specific about the exercise. Now, what obstacles may come up? How can you solve them? See the example below.

	Exercise?	Where?	When?
	biking	home to/from work (3 miles each way)	Mon, Thurs
Obstacles?	rain, cold	running late	low motivation
Solutions?	rain/cold-weather gear	prepare night before	bike with somebody

Once you do the above planning, put your plan into action and be prepared to adjust it as you go. Remember to use cues. Cues work! One study showed that a visual reminder right next to an elevator to use the stairs instead increased how many people used the stairs (Soler et al. 2010). Think of the places where you may face the choice to exercise or skip exercise and add cues to exercise if this moves you closer to what matters to you. Here are some other ways to increase your chance of being effective.

Effectiveness Hint 1: Choose an activity that gives you pleasure, such as playing a sport, dancing, or skiing, or promises a reward, such as seeing a weed-free lawn.

Effectiveness Hint 2: Make exercise an appointment. Put it into your planner to occur on specific days and at specific times.

Effectiveness Hint 3: Track your exercise to stay motivated. You can use your journal or regular planner to track when you exercise, for how long, and even what you notice afterward with regard to attention, mood, energy, and stress level (e.g., a 1 to 10 rating where 1 = super low and 10 = super high). You can even use a pedometer or a fitness app instead of pen and paper for tracking your exercise.

Effectiveness Hint 4: Have a plan B. If you schedule to play squash with somebody who then cancels, plan B may be to go for a fast walk. If you plan something outdoors and then it rains, plan B may be an indoor physical activity.

Effectiveness Hint 5: Recruit an exercise buddy, if possible.

Effectiveness Hint 6: Keep going. Excuses to avoid exercise may come easily. Just notice them without having to obey them. Dopaminize exercise and remind yourself of how you feel afterward. Also remember to notice any all-or-nothing and "what-the-hell" mind traps that come up.

If you're unconvinced that exercise is worth the effort, you may need to experience it to see the effects it has on your attention. The exercise below will show you how. Greg's worked with many individuals who were convinced by their own experience, including a law student who had difficulty understanding legal text unless he rode a stationary bike while reading.

CHALLENGE THYSELF 3 FOR EXERCISE: How Does Exercise Affect Your Attention?

How can you examine the results of your exercise on your attention? Until an objective home measure exists, we suggest being creative. To notice exercise's effects on your attention, try at least a ten-minute bout of exercise. Combine the exercise with a before-and-after test of attention. For example, try a timed two-minute mindfulness practice before and after exercising and note how many times you notice your mind wander each time. The more you notice when your mind wanders, versus having your mind wander without your noticing, the more you are regulating your attention. You are shifting it from wandering to noticing the wandering, which also brings you back to the present.

Building on Your Foundation: Mindfulness

Once you've established a strong foundation, you can aim higher. The highest you can reach, from what thousands of studies and years tell us, is to become more mindful. This is why, throughout the book, we have invited you to try small mindfulness practices. Mindfulness practice has the biggest payoff of any behavior we know after sleep, nutrition, and exercise. Mindfulness is both a trait and a skill. Some people are more mindful without intentional practice, just as some are more extraverted. Most of us, however, appear to need an intentional practice to develop the skill and, ultimately, turn it into a habit to practice.

Master of Your Mind

At UCLA's Mindful Awareness Research Center, mindfulness is defined as "paying attention to present moment experiences with openness, curiosity, and a willingness to be with what is" (http://www.marc.ucla.edu, n.d.). Some define it as nonjudgmentally paying attention to the present moment. As Tonya tells her groups, mindfulness lets you be the kind, gentle master of your mind, which goes here, there, and everywhere. You may have already noticed differences between a mindful way of being and an autopilot way of being through the smaller practices we've suggested, such as the entrance ritual at work or the mindful eating practice.

When you practice mindfulness meditations, you focus your awareness on one aspect of your present moment at a time, internal (breath, body sensations, thoughts, emotions) or external (sound, sight, smell, taste). You notice your mind's wandering and bring your mind back home, to your body. Your mind will wander, again and again, especially with low attention regulation; or anxiety, pain, or urges to do something else will intrude. This is why mindfulness is a skill, whether we are practicing it intentionally or because we possess it as a trait. Siegel (2010) and other interpersonal neurobiology scholars emphasize mindfulness as a core practice for achieving mental integration, seen as essential to well-being.

MINDFULNESS AS MIRACLE

Ever seen images of someone selling a miracle tonic, guaranteed to increase happiness, health, and even hair? Mindfulness may seem like a miracle practice. Most of the research on it has focused on depression and anxiety.

Meta-analyses—"mega-analyses" that analyze results from hundreds to thousands of subjects—show that mindfulness-based therapies decrease anxiety, depression, and physical pain and disability (e.g., Gotink et al. 2015) as well as prevent relapses of depression for those with a history of recurrent depression (Kuyken et al. 2016). But there's more to the reason we ask you to try mindfulness practice.

Research suggests that mindfulness *thickens* (*or prevents age-related thinning of*) brain areas largely responsible for attention, learning and memory, emotional flexibility, and empathy (e.g., Lazar et al. 2005; Hölzel et al. 2011). Practices such as mindfulness meditation may be a fountain of youth for our brains, albeit one we have to visit again and again (see text box).

The Fountain of Brain Youth?

(Luders, Cherbuin, & Gaser 2016)

In 2016, researchers at UCLA, the Australian National University, and the Jena University Hospital of Germany found that the brains of long-term meditators, at age 50, were an estimated seven and a half years younger than the brains of non-long-term meditators, at age 50.

They concluded that meditation may protect against age-related brain atrophy.

Mindfulness and Attention

In 2008, Zylowska and colleagues found increased attention control and reduced hyperactivity among adults and teenagers diagnosed with ADHD after two and a half hours of mindfulness training once a week for eight weeks. Two years later, Flook and colleagues (2010) looked at children's action regulation and "executive function"—meaning the mental processes that let us focus and shift attention and action, remember things such as instructions, and plan—after only 30 minutes of mindfulness training two times a week for eight weeks. They found that, with mindfulness training, both action regulation and executive function increased, with children starting with the lowest executive function showing the largest gains overall. In a recent study out of the Netherlands, adults with ADHD showed reduced symptoms of ADHD after 12 weeks of mindfulness-based cognitive therapy (Hepark et al. 2015). In a 2015 review of existing research on adult ADHD and mindfulness training, scientists concluded that mindfulness training is worth using and suggested that some "adaptations" may increase its usefulness for adults with ADHD (Mitchell, Zylowska, & Kollins 2015). We offer a practice of one mindfulness skill, which, all by itself, can transform your focus.

ADHD and Mindfulness Meditation Adaptations
(Mitchell, Zylowska, & Kollins 2015)

- Briefer practices (5–15 minutes)
- Use of walking meditations if especially restless
- Visual cues (blue sky with clouds for mindfulness of thoughts)
- Reminders (alarms, schedule into your planner)
- Inclusion of loving-kindness meditation (chapter 6 describes this)

Your Mindfulness

Are you willing to do one thing, for just this moment? Doing one thing at a time is one of several skills that define mindfulness. It's the opposite of multitasking, which our culture, to our detriment, seems to encourage. Doing one thing at a time lets you be kind to your brain. It also lets you be a rebel.

Multitasking's really repeated task-switching, which tires our brains. When we try to do more than one thing at a time, our brain switches from one task to the other. This costs us time, mistakes, and memory (American Psychological Association 2006). When you interrupt a task with another (or someone interrupts you), you have to reorient yourself to the first task when you return to it, even when you return to the task seconds later. Reorienting is like having to reread the lines of a book to remember where you left off. Medina (2014) notes that the quantifiable effects of multitasking are 50% more errors on a task along with twice as much time to accomplish it.

For someone prone to "careless mistakes," multitasking can take a major toll. Greg and Tonya have seen this up close. Greg worked with a lawyer who checked e-mail throughout the day, delaying work assignments for weeks. The lawyer estimated that he lost about a third of his possible income to multitasking. When he put limits on reading and responding to personal e-mails, his income doubled after only a month. In another technology-related example, a college student who wanted to join one of Tonya's ADHD groups looked at his phone every few seconds. During the orientation to the group, when Tonya shared what she had noticed, the student nodded, called it an "addiction," and volunteered that he had been failing classes because of it. And because of failing classes, he was unable to attend Tonya's group, which would have meant missing school. The costs of his extreme multitasking kept adding up.

You may be saying that you are an exception and focus better when you multitask. If you consider multitasking doing one thing while listening to background music or white noise, you may be right (see chapter 2). If you believe your multitasking talents go beyond this, consider the following. In 2009, researchers at Stanford University compared the performance of individuals who regularly, versus rarely, "media multitasked"— using phones and other technology to text and do things online. They found that, however they measured performance, the low multitaskers outperformed the high ones. High multitaskers were less able to ignore what was irrelevant, less able to remember what was relevant, and slower at switching from one task to another. In an interview for the *Stanford Report*, one of the researchers concluded about high multitaskers, "They're suckers for irrelevancy. Everything distracts them." Studies on non-media multitasking, such as trying to match nature pictures and being interrupted by a picture of a face, also consistently show lower performance while multitasking (e.g., Clapp, Rubens, Sabharwal, & Gazzaley 2011).

In chapter 2, we discussed how to redesign your environment for distraction control. Are you willing to try some internal distraction control?

KNOW THYSELF 3 FOR MINDFULNESS:
Measuring Multitasking

If you are willing to measure how often you multitask, first, pick *when* you will measure your multitasking. You can pick even just one day or part of one day to do this. If you multitask like crazy, one part of the day may be enough. Or you may choose to look at multitasking during a particular activity or activities, such as eating, reading, writing, conversing, cooking, gardening, or working.

Second, decide *how* you will measure multitasking. We suggest a simple count. During your chosen activity, each time you attend to a different activity, count it. For example, during a face-to-face conversation or while eating, notice each time you use your phone. Count it. You can be prepared with coins or beads put into one pocket that you will move to the other pocket, or you can jot a slash mark on paper. Be creative. Then add the count to your journal.

Third, identify *who* will track your multitasking. It may be easier to delegate. You can have someone else count your multi-tasking or consider getting an objective count of your multitasking by recording yourself. If you're at a computer, you can turn on your video to record you as you work on your computer. If you're at home, you can set up your smartphone to record you. Afterward, you can count the number of times you got on your phone, ate, or otherwise divided your attention. Also count the number of times you experienced an interruption lasting five minutes or less.

Here's an example of a way to document your multitasking (while it's happening or as you view a recording of it):

Day	Time (start/end)	Activity	Times Multitasked (0 = none, each / = 1) (notes)
Sat	7–7:30 a.m.	Reading	/ / (checked phone)
	8–8:30 a.m.	Eating	Entire time (TV)

After tracking, decide whether you want to see what difference doing one thing at a time makes using the next exercise.

CHALLENGE THYSELF 3 FOR MINDFULNESS:
Mindful-Tasking

Pick one of the activities you usually multitask. Just choose one, to start. You can try what Tonya calls mindful-tasking for other activities later.

Once you've chosen your activity, remove distractions. This may mean getting your phone out of sight and reach. If you've chosen to practice mindfulness while eating, look at distractions around the table. If you've chosen to practice while reading, look at distractions near your reading area. You are likely to reach for a habitual distraction without even realizing it—that's how much of a habit it may be. Ever catch yourself doing something that you had set aside and intended to stop doing? It happens. Better to be prepared.

Now to add other mindfulness skills to this practice, as you do one thing at a time, notice when your mind wanders away from what you are doing. Your body may follow your mind, as when your hand reaches for something that comes to your attention. Or your mind may come to realize that your body has wandered, as when you discover the bag of potato chips you moved away has shown up on your lap with your hand inside it. That's okay. Just bring your attention back to doing your one thing at a time when you notice the wandering.

Let's say you're reading and notice that your mind wanders to work. When you notice this, you can say to yourself, "My mind left to work. I'll bring it back home now, to what I am doing here." Tonya learned this from psychologist Marsha Linehan, the developer of dialectical behavior therapy and a Zen master. During a mindfulness retreat that Tonya attended, Linehan spoke of her Zen teacher Fr. Pat Hawk's practice of noticing when his mind "went for a walk" and saying, "I think I'll bring it back now." There's no need to castigate your mind for doing what it does or to put labels of "bad" or "good" on its wandering or its staying. Just notice when your mind goes for a walk and bring it back with kindness. This is the essence of mindfulness practice.

Healthy Habits and Regulation

So here you have it. You have your foundation of healthy habits and a powerful skill to build on top of these habits that will also help keep these habits going. Developing these healthy habits of your foundation and of mindfulness will transform you, if you let them—even to the level of gene expression.

As you consider these healthy habits and the others we present, we want to zoom out from the research and leave you with a big idea. The idea's inspired by Zen practice and one of Greg's favorite groups of people, the Amish. According to Donald Kraybill, co-author of *The Amish*, the Amish approach technology and other aspects of life by asking two questions: (1) "Is this going to be helpful or it is going to be detrimental?" and (2) "Is it going to bolster our life together, as a community, or is it going to somehow tear it down?" (Brady 2013). We hope that you will pause and ask these questions about all the skills we share. We think the answer to the first part of both questions, if your inner wisdom speaks, is "yes."

Before you leave this chapter, remember to give yourself time to practice its skills. Be a participant rather than just an observer. And as you read on, keep practicing this chapter's skills. Even if you stop regularly tracking healthy habits, post the tracking sheets you've filled out somewhere you can see them to have a visual reminder of the behaviors. If you stick with the skills, you'll appreciate the results.

Key Points from Chapter 3

- You are unable to change your DNA but you can change your DNA *function* by changing gene expression through your behavior.

- Our brains and bodies thrive on three behaviors: healthy eating, enough sleep, and regular exercise.

- Mindfulness practice boosts attention and action regulation.

- The *Know Thyself 3* and *Challenge Thyself 3* practices both offer opportunities to notice the connection between healthy habits and attention and action regulation.

CHAPTER 4

Attachment and Attention

Our relationships inevitably affect us. We're wired as social beings to depend on each other. It's what got us to where we are as a species. Years ago, Harry Harlow pointed this out when he said, "A lone monkey is a dead monkey." (Benjamin 2015, 44). Two scholars at Emory University described what this has come to mean for us: "It is difficult to think of any behavioural process that is more intrinsically important to us than attachment. Feeding, sleeping and locomotion are all necessary for survival, but humans are... 'a social animal' and it is our social attachments that we live for" (Insel & Young 2001, 129). Living both because of and for social attachments affects us more than we often appreciate.

Interpersonal neurobiology recognizes that we depend on others to learn to regulate ourselves and that, throughout our lives, we co-regulate each other (e.g., Schore 2001; Siegel 2010). Our brains meet and respond to one another harmoniously or otherwise. When we hear criticism or face conflict, we may want to flee, fight, or freeze, and our attention can narrow down to survival or well-being. When our survival or well-being feels threatened, it's hard to focus on much else. In other words, adjusting your attention, actions, emotions, motivation, and thoughts comes more easily when you have secure attachments to others. It becomes harder when preoccupation about abandonment consumes you, or when you fight, without your awareness, what's become part of your DNA. In this chapter, we will explore how attachment affects our attention and what we can do about it.

Consider Chuck.

Chuck came to Greg's group for adults diagnosed with ADHD because he was afraid his wife was going to leave him. She said she was tired of his forgetfulness, messiness, and poor time management. Chuck wanted his wife to attend the group with him, but she declined. The trouble with his marriage preoccupied him. Each week at group, instead of reporting on his practice of the skills, he'd report on how the stress at home made it hard to practice them. When he tried to start practicing skills, he looked at his wife's reactions, wanting reassurance of her pleasure with him. But she told him that his constant need for reassurance felt like another burden to her. Chuck felt even more worried that she no longer loved him and began drinking more and more to relieve his anxiety.

Chuck's fears of losing his wife narrowed his attention. His focus on interpreting his wife's responses to him as "staying or leaving" decreased his ability to adjust his attention and actions.

Now that we've looked at how you relate to your environment and how you relate to yourself, we focus this chapter on how you relate to others. In looking at how relationships matter for your attention and action regulation, we will extend your exterior-interior matching practice to social relationships. We'll start with some background—some "strange" studies on infants and mothers that show what it means to love and be loved—and then move to the fascinating ways that relationships from childhood on speak to our DNA, to us as social beings, and to our brains. Finally, we'll describe what you can do to develop your relationships for optimal self-regulation. After all, we all seek relationships that contribute to our well-being. Sometimes we just need help knowing what they look like and how to attain them.

The Emotional Ties That Bind Us: Infant Love

Let's go back to the 1960s, a time of thought-provoking social and scientific experiments. A psychologist named Mary Ainsworth designed a method, called "the strange situation," to study infants' attachment to their caregivers. In a nutshell, "attachment" refers to the enduring affection that binds one human being to another. The strange situation consists of a sequence of three-minute "episodes" designed to reveal what attachment looks like. During each episode, researchers observed how infants responded to their mothers' (and later fathers' and other caregivers') and a stranger's alternating presence and absence.

From the strange situation (and other) studies, we learned quite a bit. First, we learned that infants develop different attachment styles depending on how their parents or caregivers respond to them. These styles may be:

- *Secure*, which is related to empathetic, consistently available and nurturing caregiving; or

- *Insecure*, which is related to inconsistent, insensitive caregiving and shows up as an attachment style described as:

  - *avoidant* (seen with an emotionally unavailable, rejecting caregiver),

  - *anxious/ambivalent* (seen with an inconsistently available caregiver who meets the infant's needs unpredictably), or

- *disorganized* (seen when a caregiver is a source of terror, or is abusive).

We also learned that insecure attachments either fragment attention or narrow it. If infants are unable to count on being loved and kept safe by a caregiver, their attention (and behavior) fragments between approaching and avoiding the caregiver. If infants can count on the *absence* of love and safety from a caregiver, their attention turns to avoiding the caregiver. And if they can count on terror and danger from a caregiver, they appear to have no safe place for their attention to turn, and they "check out" or become angry. Secure attachments, where love and safety form the tie between infant and caregiver, offer infants the freedom to shift their attention to where it's needed. And this freedom is the essence of regulation, whether of attention or another aspect of self.

As Siegel (1999) writes, attachment works as a crucial way by which "the self" regulates. Siegel sees attachment as one of the functions of our minds on which our well-being depends. So from an interpersonal neurobiology perspective, it makes sense for a primary target of therapy to be moving toward a secure attachment, if this is missing. And from an attention and action regulation perspective, it makes sense for attachment to be a primary target for increasing this regulation. When our social resources are ample, both attention and action appear easier to us.

By looking at attachment relationships and attention over the lifespan, we know that secure attachments help us to shift our attention with flexibility and to adjust our behaviors as needed. Researchers around the world have shown this. Italian researchers found this with toddlers, whose secure attachments to child care center caregivers were related to their ability to shift their attention from one activity to another while at the child care centers (Pallini & Laghi 2012), and with four- and five-year-olds, who performed better on several attention and concentration tasks when they had secure attachments (Commodari 2013). In the United States, teachers rated children 9, 12, and 15 years of age on attentiveness, and researchers found that the children rated as more attentive were the ones with secure attachments (Jacobsen & Hoffman 1997).

Attachment Relationships Leave Their Mark

After extensive focus on infant attachment, researchers turned their attention to early childhood and then older ages until, eventually, reaching adulthood. And they found that, through all these stages, attachment was crucial. In fact, our early experiences with caregivers and the ways these experiences teach us to attach to others leave chemical marks on our genes, as recent studies have shown. We'll look at those studies now.

Let's go deep into your interior, to your DNA. We need only travel back to the start of this century, where we find studies on *DRD4*, a dopamine receptor gene seen as one of the gene mutations that contribute to variations of ADHD. In Finland, researchers followed 92 children from childhood to adulthood for over 14 years to understand the influence of childhood environment on *DRD4*'s effect on novelty-seeking behavior. They found that having versions of *DRD4* was associated with a higher chance of extreme novelty seeking for adults when their childhood family environments were more "hostile" (defined by emotional distance, little tolerance of normal child activity, and strict discipline—an environment likely to contribute to insecure attachment) (Keltikangas-Järvinen et al. 2004, 308). Adults who had the same gene mutations and more nurturing early family environments showed, overall, a low level of novelty seeking, suggesting "that the childhood environment had the potential to negate the genotypic predisposition" (310).

Other studies have shown the same kind of interaction between genetic disposition and early family environment when looking specifically at symptoms of ADHD. For example, a study led by a researcher at the University of New Orleans found that versions of the DRD4 gene increased children's chance of being diagnosed with ADHD *only* when these children had inconsistent parenting (Martel et al. 2011). Then just a few years ago, German researchers found that adolescents who had a DRD4 gene mutation showed more symptoms of ADHD when they had experienced less sensitive, stimulating maternal care at *infancy* (Nikitopoulos et al. 2014).

In all three studies, a less nurturing childhood family environment seemed to set the stage for DRD4 to have more powerful effects on ADHD symptoms. But we must be careful with our interpretations. None showed a *causal* link between parenting and ADHD. It's hard to isolate parenting and ADHD symptoms from other factors that may be causes of both. Also, there likely are reciprocal relationships at play, where a child's genes influence parenting and parenting influences these genes. Consider a Danish study that followed over 75,000 mothers and their infants up to 14 years to identify early factors associated with a childhood diagnosis of ADHD. The study revealed that, among other early factors, when mothers reported finding their 18-month-old infants hard to handle, these infants had a higher chance, albeit a small one, of having a clinical diagnosis of ADHD at 8 to 14 years of age (Lemcke et al. 2016).

What these studies point to is the need for researchers to consider early family environments as they seek to illuminate the gene-environment interactions that give rise to the variations of ADHD. And they point to there being no need for these family environments to be especially harsh or inconsistent, given that the dopamine receptor gene mutation seems to confer *sensitivity* to the family environment. Remember the finding on lead exposure (see chapter 1)? The blood levels of lead were at a "safe" level, reminding us that when it comes to environmental causes, a little may go a long way, given the right genes.

Whatever the exact nature of the relationship between ADHD and attachment, researchers recently reviewing 29 studies on the matter concluded that the association between the two seems quite clear (Storebø, Rasmussen, & Simonsen 2016). And what you may care about most is that the review indicated that adults with ADHD have a higher rate of insecure attachment. Dutch researchers, for example, found that, among adults who had recently been diagnosed with ADHD, only about 20% of them had a secure attachment compared with 59% of the general population of the Netherlands (Koemans et al. 2015).

In the United States, the research on adults' attachment, attention, and action focuses on all things emotional, including positive and negative feelings, thoughts, facial expressions, and social interactions. In the emotional realm, secure attachment means flexibility of attention, and insecure attachment means rigidity. We'll tell you about just one study on this. In 2012, researchers measured the brain activity of three groups of participants—showing either a secure, anxious, or avoidant attachment pattern—as they viewed positive, negative, and neutral emotional images of people (Chavis & Kisley 2012). The anxious and avoidant attachment groups showed biased attention. The anxious paid more attention to positive emotional images and the avoidant paid more attention to negative ones. Only the secure attachment group played no favorites and could pay equal attention to positive and negative images.

Secure attachment creates the right conditions for the development of self-regulation. We can see this through observation of the middle prefrontal cortex of your brain. Here, the brain outcomes of secure attachment, as Dan Siegel (2012a) notes, include:

- flexible behaviors (such as the ability to pause before acting and evaluate options),

- regulation of body,

- regulation of emotions,

- attuned communication,

- empathy,

- insight/self-awareness,

- decreased conditioned fear, and

- morality.

These outcomes fit the perspective that attachment influences our attention and action regulation.

Shifting to Security

Both early-life and late-life relationships influence our attachment patterns and attention regulation. Our brains respond to experience from before we're born to the moment we die. As long as we're alive, there's no such thing as too late. There's only more effort needed sometimes.

We know of a few ways to shift from insecure to secure attachments. First, know yourself. Does your core way of relating to others create an optimal environment for attention regulation and well-being?

KNOW THYSELF 4: What's Your Attachment Style?

To identify your attachment style, we recommend a well-researched measure called the Relationship Structures (ECR-RS) Questionnaire (Fraley et al. 2011). We have included the ECR-RS for you below along with its somewhat complicated scoring instructions. (If you prefer, you can also find the ECR-RS online, where you can have it scored for you, at http://www.yourpersonality.net/relstructures.)

Please read each of the following statements and rate the extent to which you believe each statement best describes your feelings about close relationships generally. Use a 7-point scale where 1 = strongly disagree and 7 = strongly agree. (We kept the statements unaltered, to keep them faithful to the researched measure.)

1. It helps to turn to people in times of need.

2. I usually discuss my problems and concerns with others.

3. I talk things over with people.

4. I find it easy to depend on others.

5. I don't feel comfortable opening up to others.

6. I prefer not to show others how I feel deep down.

7. I often worry that other people do not really care for me.

8. I'm afraid that other people may abandon me.

9. I worry that others won't care about me as much as I care about them.

Now to score it:

First, change the scores of statements 1 through 4 using the rows of numbers below. For example, if you had a rating of 3, change your 3 to a 5 and if you had a 6, change it to a 2.

Your number:	1	2	3	4	5	6	7
Revised number:	7	6	5	4	3	2	1

Next, average your ratings for statements 1 through 6 (using the revised numbers you got for 1 to 4) and, separately, average your ratings for statements 7 through 9. The first average gives you your avoidance score and the second average gives you your anxiety score. Together, they reveal your attachment style, as follows.

Both low (4.5 or lower) = relatively secure

Anxiety high and avoidance low = relatively preoccupied

Avoidance high and anxiety low = relatively dismissing

Both high (4.5 or higher) = relatively rare style of preoccupation *and* dismissal

Got your adult attachment style? Let's move on.

Adult attachment styles, like childhood styles, fall into two categories, secure and insecure attachment, and three subcategories of insecure attachment. Only the names of these subcategories change. What's called avoidant attachment during childhood is called *dismissing*, what's called anxious/ambivalent is renamed *preoccupied*, and what's disorganized translates into *unresolved*.

In a nutshell, a secure adult attachment style means that you find it easy to be close to others. An insecure attachment style means a, b, or c:

a. *Dismissing:* you undervalue relationships and keep others away by avoiding intimacy (you are an island— no one depends on you and you depend on no one),

b. *Preoccupied:* you want to be close to others but worry about whether others want to be close to you and fear being hurt, or

c. *Unresolved:* you may dissociate and struggle with psychopathology.

Each attachment style comes with different ways of relating to others, as you might imagine, and has different consequences for attention and action regulation—which is to say your ADHD (remember that ADHD is low attention and action regulation). What we find especially fascinating is how insecure attachments absorb your attention and energy, one way or another. With a preoccupied attachment, you are hyperattentive to attachment cues (Dewitte et al. 2007). So questions of love, trust, and loyalty may dominate your attention. Someone's late arrival, delayed reply, or declined invitation can consume you, leading to rumination that makes it hard for you to pay attention, or to despair that keeps you from acting. With a dismissing attachment, your brain dims your conscious attention to your intimacy needs (Edelstein 2006). "I'm better off on my own" or "Who needs them?" might be your mantra.

When you're comfortable being close to others and free of intense fear of losing them, you can pay attention to what's around you with more flexibility. This gives you more freedom when it comes to your actions. In other words, secure attachment increases attention and action regulation—that is, it decreases your symptoms of ADHD (e.g., Bergin & Bergin 2009). And research suggests that your attachment pattern matters across environments, including affecting your job performance (e.g., Neustadt, Chamorro-Premuzic, & Furnham 2011) and behavior (Richards & Schat 2011).

Over recent years, researchers have linked different attachment patterns to different patterns of brain activity (Vrtička & Vuilleumier 2012) and different physiological responses. Compared with individuals with secure attachments, for example, individuals with preoccupied and dismissing attachments show more intense fight-or-flight responses under stressful social situations, such as relationship conflict (Pietromonaco & Powers 2015). Researchers have also linked attachment differences to dopamine receptor genes. Consider a study of salespeople. Researchers found that salespeople with avoidant attachment styles who possessed specific variations of *DRD2* and *DRD4*—the same dopamine receptor genes associated with ADHD—showed greater customer orientation (Verbeke, Bagozzi, & van den Berg 2014).

To see how an attachment-stress connection matters to your attention and action regulation, remember the last time you were super stressed. What happened to your attention and action?

If you have an insecure adult attachment style, you have plenty of company...try about 41% of the US population (about 25% dismissing, 11% preoccupied, and 5% unresolved) (Mickelson, Kessler, and Shaver 1997). But here's the thing: Of the 59% with a secure attachment, some of them carried a secure attachment from childhood into adulthood and some "earned" a secure attachment—gaining it through later experiences of a secure attachment or through making sense of earlier experiences (more on this soon). And, when you have a secure attachment, overall, there appears to be no way to tell from how you act whether you've had a secure attachment all along or earned it (Saunders et al. 2011). The possible exception to this appears to be for symptoms of depression, with those possessing an earned secure attachment found to have a higher chance of symptoms of depression than those with what's called a "continuous" secure attachment (Pearson et al. 1994). Perhaps given the overall lack of differences, however, even brain research investigating secure versus insecure attachments ignores whether a secure attachment was earned later during life or present throughout (e.g., Lenzi et al. 2015).

So, if you have an insecure attachment, let's start with the direct path to an earned secure attachment. Whatever your age, experiencing a close relationship with someone who is securely attached increases your chance of developing a secure attachment. Secure attachment is an experience rather than an event. You have to feel it. Your brain needs to feel it. There's no need for it to be a romantic close relationship. It could, for example, be a close relationship with a friend, teacher, therapist, or mentor. And it can be a brief one rather than a relationship that continues over the course of your life.

There are also indirect paths to an earned secure attachment. One is through how you see your past. You are unable to change the facts of your past, but you can change how you interpret them and, by doing so, change how they affect you. The other path involves targeting the brain outcomes of secure attachment: flexible behaviors, regulation of body, regulation of emotions, attuned communication, empathy, insight/self-awareness, decreased conditioned fear, and morality. If you possess an insecure attachment pattern, you can develop the outcomes of secure attachment by *activating* the parts of your middle prefrontal cortex that your early relationships left underdeveloped (Siegel 2010).

CHALLENGE THYSELF 4: Shift Toward Security

The direct way to shift toward security is to experience a close relationship with someone securely attached. Finding someone who qualifies requires time, of course.

If you and a beloved are both insecurely attached, you can consider couples therapy that targets attachment, such as emotion-focused therapy. Emotion-focused therapy emphasizes secure attachments and experiences of security, with research offering evidence of its effectiveness (e.g., Denton et al. 2000). You or you and your beloved can also use indirect ways to shift toward security.

The indirect way consists of two paths.

Path 1: Reflect on and make sense of your childhood experiences. Understand how things happened without having to approve of, or agree with, what happened. Just try to understand the pieces of the puzzle and their influences on you. Remember, everything has a cause. You can make sense of your experiences growing up by creating a clear, coherent story about the causes, seen and unseen, of your caregivers' behavior and yours. The causes are the chain of events, including unwanted ones, that logically led to what happened. Piecing these possible causes together into a coherent, meaningful story may seem a scary endeavor for some. But it's worth it because it opens up the possibility for a secure attachment pattern to emerge. According to Siegel (2012a), it does this by organizing the brain. Siegel describes the organization as neural integration of different areas of the brain: building neglected bridges so thoughts, emotions, senses, and behavior can access each other. The best way that we know to embark on this integration enterprise is through the Adult Attachment Interview (AAI), conducted by a mental health therapist who knows how to do it (Siegel 2010). If you have an insecure attachment pattern, you may be able to make sense of your past through other means than the AAI and with someone other than a therapist; we just have no formula we can give you for this.

Making sense of your past depends on the stories you tell about your life and what experiences and insights influence these stories.

Path 2: *Practice targeted mindfulness.* Mindfulness practice strengthens the same functions of the brain that secure attachment strengthens. "Targeted" mindfulness practice focuses on increasing a particular brain function—for example, emotion regulation—by increasing awareness of an experience tied to the brain function. What you increase your awareness of depends on what kind of insecure style of attachment you have.

- For a dismissing style of attachment, one thing you can do to shift toward security is to develop your awareness of your body sensations and emotions. A dismissing style of attachment dims this awareness.

- Preoccupied style? Develop your awareness of what soothes and calms you to free your attention from fear.

- An unresolved style may require working with a therapist to develop awareness of both the here and now and the there and then to notice when you experience the past as the present. There are multiple ways to do this, which include breath awareness and imagery of a safe place.

Continue the exercise as long as you need. Your practice with shifting to security, if you need to do so, will lay the groundwork for the specific work on communication and connection that the next chapter presents.

Insecure Attachment Patterns: What's Missing?

Dismissing

Behind the devaluing of relationships—"Who needs them?"—is little awareness of your own body sensations and emotions, which are communicating, "*You* need them." Think thoughts cut off from feelings.

Preoccupied

The fear of losing somebody draws your attention to the other person for reassurance and leaves you less aware of how to calm and soothe yourself. Think painful feelings cut off from self-soothing.

Unresolved

Reactive, automatic pilot flight-fight-freeze responses break your connection to your thoughts and to seeing differences between the present and past. Think body sensations and feelings cut off from thought.

Our brains are wired for relationships. Psychologist Louis Cozolino (2013) points out that our brains have evolved to pay attention to the behaviors and emotions of other people. Secure attachments enable regulation of this attention and of attention, generally, because they let us experience safety, connection, empathy, and soothing. As Sue Johnson, PhD, the creator of emotion-focused therapy, puts it, "when you feel safe inside your own skin, with your own emotions and with another person, that's when you can really engage, and explore, the environment" (NICABM 2016, 4:08). Research shows that, from such safety, we are open to caring for others and, indeed, give them more compassion and help (Mikulincer et al. 2005). In the next chapter, we begin to build on this foundation with specific skills to connect and communicate.

Key Points from Chapter 4

- Developing a secure attachment can increase your ability to regulate your attention and action.

- Know your core ways of relating to others and how to move toward changing these ways, if needed, through *Know Thyself 4* and *Challenge Thyself 4*.

CHAPTER 5

Communication and Connection

As social beings, we are more than wired to pay attention to other people—we are also wired to derive happiness from sharing our lives with them. Deriving happiness from our connections with one another is one way to get us to pay attention to each other.

The way you pay attention to others and communicate with them affects your chances of deriving happiness from your relationships and getting what you want out of your social interactions. After all, relationships and interactions are mutually created rather than just "joined." And here's where it can get tough when attention and action regulation are low. Distractibility, forgetfulness, and low impulse control, among other symptoms of low attention and action regulation, tend to interfere with communication and connection.

The degree to which low attention and action regulation interferes with communication and connection varies from relatively slight to extreme. We have seen members of our groups who connect well with others and only struggle with remembering what they wanted to say for a particular social situation. For example, it's common for us to hear such things as, "I went to see my doctor to talk about my sleep. As soon as she asked how I was doing, I began talking about my recent trip and other things. I forgot to mention sleep before I left." We have also seen members with more extreme struggles to communicate and to connect. They speak many words without leaving their audience clear about their intended message and may themselves even forget their intended message over the course of talking. They lose their audience and get lost themselves. They may also interrupt others more than they or others would like. Whether the struggle's relatively slight or serious, one of the most popular requests we hear is for relationship and communication skills. It is largely thanks to these requests that we have included these skills.

In this chapter, we present skills to regulate your attention and action during communication so that you can connect with others more often, as well as specific connection and communication skills that show you where to put your attention as a conversation is happening. We have heard from several of our group members that even when they can focus, they struggle with figuring out what to focus on. In this chapter, we offer several ways you can better anchor your attention, as listener and as speaker.

KNOW THYSELF 5: How Do You Connect and Communicate?

Have you ever had the opportunity to observe, from a distance, how you interact with others? If you'd like to do this, there are creative ways that you can. One way is to videorecord an interaction, ideally with the permission of all involved, or have someone else do this. If you ask someone to do this for a conversation without telling you which conversation will be recorded, you might even act more as you usually do. Afterward, you could view the recording and notice, just by counting, how many times you looked at the other person and/or interrupted. If you are curious, time how long you spoke before pausing and compare this to how much time passed before the other person paused. If a video recording seems too much to you, try an audio recording only to listen to elements of interest to you such as interruptions.

Get your journal and see if you can create a chart for counting a behavior of interest. An easy one to start could be interrupting. On the left side of your paper, write the behavior or behaviors of interest. Underneath this will be where you count how many times you exhibit them. Now if you want to see how these behaviors, such as your interruptions, influence the conversation, note others' responses on the right side of the paper. What responses do you want to notice? Other people's eye contact? Their facial expressions? Let's say you want to see whether, at the moment you interrupt, people look at you, away, or down. Then on the right, across from each slash mark representing an interruption, write "looked away" or "looked at" or "looked down." Here's an example for one five-minute conversation where the observer counted ten interruptions.

In conversations, how much do I...	How do others respond?
Interrupt?	
/ / / / / / / / / / (5-min chat)	stop talking, look down, ask me to wait, sigh, say that what I am thinking will change once they're finished

Later, expand this exercise to other behaviors on your side and to other kinds of responses, as needed. You may look at "engagement" versus "disengagement" as a response, for example. You can also look at the practice of communication and connection skills, as you learn them.

Descriptions from Tonya's ADHD group members about *seeing* the way they communicate have included "mind-blowing." They speak about the powerful effect of seeing what they have only heard from others. One member said he'd heard he had a habit of never finishing sentences and he thought others exaggerated this until, by videotaping, he had a chance to hear it for himself. He said it changed the way he spoke. He now finishes sentences. It's really hard to hear and see how we communicate while we communicate. You may find observation mind-blowing. And if you think you'll be on your best behavior and a videotaped conversation will show an artificial you, just fast-forward about five minutes into the conversation.

If you find recording a conversation unappealing, you can focus on one aspect of a conversation and choose a way to count this one thing. When Tonya wants to count something, such as the number of judgments that come to her mind, she wears a counter that's for golfers to count their strokes. It consists of balls on a string that she can raise one at a time. Another way to count your behavior of interest, which Tonya heard about during one of her group sessions, is through a pocket full of pennies. You can put the pennies into your right pocket (or left, if you're left-handed) and then move them one at a time to your other pocket. Of course, you could also ask your listener to be the counter and to count discreetly, such as under a table, if you'd find this more useful.

Once you've practiced identifying how you communicate and noticing whether you'd like to change something about this—for example, staying on point more often or interrupting less frequently—turn to the skills that follow. As you read, you can focus on skills that target the change(s) you desire.

Skills as the Listener

If you want to show others that they matter to you, stay alert when they talk to you and really listen. To stay alert, it will first help to practice the sleep skills from the chapter on healthy habits and then to practice listening. To practice listening so that you stay alert when you are really bored or restless when someone's speaking, instead of turning your attention away, turn it more fully to the speaker. Most times, you are likely to find that the speaker has become much more interesting.

Attending and participating as fully as possible, even if only as a listener, can at the very least decrease your boredom and restlessness. Dr. Linehan (2003) tells a story of feeling restless at church and thinking that the priest just kept going on and on as the minutes passed slowly. Bored to the extreme and feeling stuck up front where it was harder to exit quietly, she decided to fully throw herself into being at church listening to the priest, without judgments (of being unable to stand it, of the priest being boring, and so on). By the end, when the priest finished, she'd become so engaged with listening that it seemed as if time had just flown by. You may have had a similar experience.

Listening relies on attention regulation. You need to *stop* paying attention to something else, including your own meandering mind; *shift* your attention to what someone's saying to you both verbally and nonverbally; *start* attending to what they are saying; and try to *sustain* your attention. To do this, first commit to practicing listening. How much time you commit depends on the situation, what you want out of it, and how much time you're willing to give to the practice. Starting with less time and working up to more is likely to be more effective than planning a marathon listening session.

In the thick of a conversation, the skills that follow will increase your attention and action regulation from moment to moment.

Stop, Look, and Listen Mindfully

In your next conversation, once you've committed to practicing listening, stop. Stop whatever else you are doing that's nonessential. Stop multitasking. Put away your phone and other distractions. The idea is to get what's irrelevant at the moment out of sight, out of mind. At the moment, these are your flashing lights. Then you need to get what's relevant in sight, in mind: the other person, a guiding light at the moment.

To get someone in sight, in mind, you literally see them. Shift your attention to the other person using your eyes, ears, and mind. Hearing someone's words and tone of voice is only part of listening. A lot of communication happens nonverbally through facial expressions and body language. If you miss the nonverbal communication, you may miss the most crucial elements of what someone's communicating to you. You may also miss opportunities to connect most meaningfully to somebody. We are wired to give more weight to what others express nonverbally than to the words that come out of their mouths. But, as we've heard from our groups, sometimes it's hard for you to notice—your attention's elsewhere. If someone says, "I'm fine" with a neutral tone while you are gazing elsewhere, you will register that they are fine despite the fact that their nostrils are flaring and their arms are crossed as they stare intently away from you. Had you been looking, your brain would have registered that the person seemed less than "fine." When what we see conflicts with what we hear, our brains override what we hear with what we see. As Medina (2014) says, "Vision trumps all other senses." You need to see a speaker's nonverbal behavior to get the speaker's message most clearly, and sometimes even to get the *real* message. So looking as part of listening shows others that you are trying to pay attention and increases the chances that you'll really hear them.

Okay, you've got your eyes and ears turned toward your target and your mind wanders off. It refuses to follow along. Then what? This brings us to the final part of Stop, Look, and Listen Mindfully. First, to listen mindfully, accept that a wandering mind is actually normal, even when undesired. In the United States, our minds wander nearly half the time we're awake. Add low attention regulation to a wandering-prone mind, and this percentage is likely higher. After all, it's part of the nature of the beast when it comes to low attention regulation. When you accept that your mind's a wanderer, you move closer to listening mindfully. Only by accepting something can we change it or learn to work with it.

The second part of listening mindfully is noticing where your mind is when you are having a conversation. Is it on the conversation or has it left? When you notice that it's wandered off, bring your attention back, with kindness and without judgment. Your attention's just doing what it does. It needs you to guide it to where it needs to be at the moment by noticing what it does and bringing it back, again and again. Bring it back without an evaluation of you or your attention as "good" or "bad." This is the nonjudgmental part of mindfulness.

When you practice listening mindfully, you practice being nonjudgmental toward your mind's wandering, yourself, and others and what they communicate to you. We are often quick to evaluate things that are subjective as good or bad, right or wrong. And we are quick to layer interpretations on top of what we observe. Here are some examples:

- When we have the thought that someone is "ugly," we are usually adding, by our choice of this word, an evaluation that there's something bad about their looks (rather than offering an objective description of the facts).

- When we say someone "meant" to hurt our feelings, we are layering their behavior (say, of canceling a get-together) with an interpretation of their intent.

In the first example, the fact may simply be that we dislike how someone's nose looks. If we are practicing being nonjudgmental, we notice the judgment "ugly" and turn it into a description of facts (for a face, what we can see). In the second example, the person who canceled could have one of many reasons for doing so (such as having a work deadline to meet, or having just had an argument) other than an intent to hurt us. Anchor your attention to what you can actually observe. This can keep the flashing lights of your mind from turning on so that you can *sustain* your attention on what someone's actually saying and doing.

Paraphrase

It's one thing to listen to somebody and another to show that person you've listened. Your eye contact and other non-verbal communication show you're physically present. But because most of us know that our minds can wander during a conversation even if our eyes and bodies stay put, you may also want to demonstrate your mental presence. If you want to show somebody that you have been listening mindfully and, therefore, brought your attention back when it wandered, paraphrase what they said.

When you paraphrase, you use your own words to express the meaning of what someone said. By paraphrasing, you have a chance to show that you're listening *and* check whether you're understanding. Usually, when someone says something as brief and simple as, "I'm cold. I'd like the windows to stay closed," there's no need to paraphrase by saying, for example, "You'd like me to stop opening the windows." You could show that you listened mindfully just by saying, "Got it. I'll close them." When the message is more complicated or involves multiple ideas, experiences, or requests, then paraphrase. The act of paraphrasing will direct your attention, and let someone else redirect it, if needed, to the essence of what someone said. Paraphrasing will also increase your chance of remembering what someone said and regulating your action, if required.

CHALLENGE THYSELF 5 FOR LISTENING, PART 1:
Practice Paraphrasing

Practice paraphrasing with someone close to you. When she or he says something to you that involves two or more ideas, requests, and/ or experiences, give a brief recap of what was said so that she or he knows you listened. Or paraphrase when you simply find what's being said confusing or hard to follow. Request feedback on whether the speaker felt understood. Keep practicing to develop the skill. Until you become used to it, you may feel awkward. And your speaker, if unaccustomed to hearing paraphrasing from you, may even ask what you're doing. Surf the urge to give up.

Surf the Urge to Interrupt

Action regulation comes into play various ways during communication. Of the four S's, *stopping* may be the one most needed when you have low action regulation, because with low action regulation comes low impulse control. And low impulse control can give rise to interrupting (as well as talking excessively, which we'll address under speaker skills). The problem with interrupting is that part of ensuring you get other people's intended messages is to let them express these messages. If you're an interrupter, you may find that you're missing what others are trying to say to you.

When you stop and pay attention to your interruptions, you will notice something really useful about them. Before your interruption is an interruption, it's an urge. You feel a strong desire to speak up while others are talking. Your thought may seem to matter so much when it flies through your head, you want to send it out into the world at that moment. Here's the thing: Only some thoughts need to get out into the world. Others are okay forgotten. Even if the thought has its time and place to be said, the time and place may be later and somewhere else. Overall, the cons of interrupting often outweigh the pros of speaking the thought. Urge surfing involves mindfulness skills (Walsh, n.d.), so if you've been practicing the skills you learned as you read chapter 2, you may have a head start.

Urges to act are like waves. They go up and up and up until they level out and then go down. Often, we obey our urges by the time they get to the top of the wave because the going down happens more quickly, as, for example, with the urge to interrupt and the immediate relief of interrupting. But urges, again like waves, come and go. If you, instead, surf an urge by observing it nonjudgmentally, it will go away—more gradually, perhaps, but it will go away. We add "nonjudgmentally" because one way to increase the chance you will obey an urge is to have judgments about it, such as seeing the urge as "unbearable." Urges are bearable, if we give them the chance. Urge surfing's a skill that came out of work on addictions. If someone who smokes can surf the urge to light a cigarette, you can surf an urge to interrupt, with practice.

CHALLENGE THYSELF 5 FOR LISTENING, PART 2:
Urge Surfing

In your next conversation give urge surfing (or, as Tonya's husband Sergio calls it, "urge suffering") a try. Afterward, reflect on what the conversation was like for you and appeared to be like for the other person. If you keep practicing this skill, you may hear from others what they are noticing about conversations with you being different, depending on how much you already urge surf.

- Urge surfing starts with mindfulness. You have to notice an urge without judgment, without trying to fight it or change it, to surf it.

- You can prepare for urge surfing before you enter a conversation by being mindful. Notice your breath to start, letting the breath breathe itself. When something pulls your attention away from the breath, gently bring your attention back.

- During a conversation, notice when the urge to interrupt arises. Notice how this urge affects your body. Where do you feel it? Multiple places? Focus on one at a time. What is happening there? Notice the sensations and everything you can about them, including their shape, intensity, and changes, particularly with your inhale and exhale. Notice any judgments (such as "It's unbearable") and gently bring your attention back to the urge with curiosity about it.

- You can use the practice to surf other urges before surfing an urge to interrupt. Start with one of your less intense urges and then, once you've built a little urge surfing muscle, move on to a more intense urge.

If mindfully surfing the urge to express a thought proves overwhelming because, for example, you fear forgetting it, try this: See whether your thoughts need to be shared as urgently as you feel they do during a conversation by writing them down when someone's talking. Then, when it's your speaking turn, look at these thoughts to see whether they need to be said as much as your urge indicated. Tonya had a group member who often interrupted and said he *had to* because of the weight of his thoughts. She asked him to write his thoughts down (she had learned this from Greg). One day when she asked him what thoughts on his list he wanted to share, he said that by writing down his thoughts he'd discovered that it was the sense of urgency that had compelled his interruptions rather than the relevance of the thoughts themselves. You'll often find that if you surf your urge to interrupt, you'll be able to see your thoughts and their need to be said more clearly.

When you surf an urge, including the urge to interrupt, you notice the urge without acting on it. It's an action regulation skill—a way to *stop* an action.

Skills as the Speaker

Even if you can really listen to somebody and let them know this, you also want to be able to communicate *what* you intend to communicate. When you speak, you want others to be interested and to stay interested, right? We bet you'd like others to be willing to see your point of view, even if they disagree with it. Attention and action regulation can keep you focused on *what you say, how much you say,* and *how* you say what you want to say so that others are open to your message and receive it.

Pay Attention to Your Audience

One day, Tonya and her son were on a walk. Her son, who is diagnosed with ADHD, had been talking nonstop for about ten minutes when they encountered construction that was much louder. At this point, he turned to her and said, "Okay, hold on. I can't hear you." Tonya had been silent the entire time they'd been walking and was struck by the possibility that her son had thought they were actually having a *conversation.* Weeks later, she met up for lunch with an acquaintance who is diagnosed with ADHD. Her acquaintance spoke the entire hour they were together, with Tonya nodding and trying to interject a word or two here and there. At the end of the lunch, her acquaintance said, "It was great talking with you." Tonya was reminded of what her son had said to her weeks prior. Both experiences reminded her that paying attention to your audience is a skill. Tonya and Greg have both noticed members of their ADHD groups who speak without attending to their audience.

When you pay attention to your audience, you do more than look at them. You *notice* them. You notice their facial expressions and body language. Does your audience look interested, confused, or bored? What does their body language express? Are they leaning toward you, looking relaxed, or moving away and tense? In our culture, we tend to lean toward somebody when we're interested and to nod and say "um-hum" to show engagement. If someone's turning away, trying to get up to go, remaining standing when sitting's possible, or holding on to a doorknob, then this person's likely trying to disengage from the conversation. If the person you're talking to keeps opening and closing his mouth, this person likely wants to speak.

Paying attention to your audience can sometimes be a hard skill to practice. You may be afraid to notice that others are confused, bored, or losing interest while you're speaking. If you expect an unwanted response from your audience, or fear becoming distracted by facial expressions, you may avoid looking at them. We advise noticing what thoughts and emotions keep you from paying attention to your audience without acting on these. Unless you see the response, how will you know whether you are connecting and whether you need to change direction to prevent disconnecting or to reconnect?

CHALLENGE THYSELF 5 FOR SPEAKING, PART 1:
STOP

To notice how a conversation is going and whether you are still present for it, practice STOP. It's one of the mindfulness practices Dr. Zylowska (2012) prescribes to regulate attention during communication. Here's how it works:

Stop.

Take a Breath.

Observe: Where's your attention? Is it on the audience and the topic at hand?

Proceed: If you are distracted, return to the audience and topic and then proceed.

During STOP, you can also observe your thoughts, feelings, and body sensations. You can notice judgments and whether your thoughts and feelings pull your attention away from your intended communication or keep you focused on it. If your feelings pull you away, label them to help free up your attention. Try this during your next conversation.

Describe

Paying attention to your audience is a start to communicating and connecting effectively. Another part of your job as a communicator is to be clear. It's hard to connect with others when we are unclear about our experiences and perspectives. The best way we know how to achieve clarity is to describe our experiences (what we know through our senses and observation of thoughts and emotions). Dr. Linehan (2014) defines describing as a skill of mindfulness. When you describe, you convey what you know by observing your experiences: bodily, emotional, and mental.

In our society, we often focus on time—the lack of it—and how to get places and do things faster and faster. Our communication gets faster and faster, with text messages, Twitter, emoticons, and thumbs up and down. We have reduced many phrases to three and four letters, and emotions to an expressive yellow circle. When we speak with each other, we rely on judgments, which are shortcuts for expressing whether we like or dislike something, or whether we consider something to have desired or undesired consequences. We say things are "good," we are "fine," our day was "horrible," or what someone said was "terrible." We hardly get to our actual experiences. Description is expressing the facts of your experiences. Instead of calling what someone said "terrible," we'd say, for example, that it hurt us. Description, as a skill, involves staying away from evaluative judgments and interpretations. It's effective communication and encourages connection.

When you practice describing, you notice judgments and turn them into descriptions (Linehan 2014). Let's give you an example of something that comes up often and may seem a funny one. This sentence expresses two judgments: "You have bad manners and should chew with your mouth closed." Did you spot the judgments? "Bad" and "should"? Go ahead and try to turn the sentence about manners into a description and then read our conversion. Here's ours: "When you chew with your mouth open, I become distracted by what I see and hear. I'd really appreciate it if you would chew with your mouth closed." Now we get that you may just let someone chew with an open mouth, even if this bothers you. What we hope you're seeing is that judgments pretend to be the truth about reality, whereas descriptions convey your experience of reality. Try turning judgments into descriptions and noticing whether, at the moment that you do, this changes how you feel about the person or situation you were judging. Also notice how much less distracting descriptions are compared with judgments, negative or positive.

Stop Burying the Lead

Another part of your job as an effective communicator is to avoid losing your own train of thought. The best way to do this that we know is to borrow from schools of journalism, which teach journalists to avoid "burying the lead." When you communicate, you need to have a "lead," a main message that you want to convey. And avoid losing your lead.

There are different ways that your lead can get lost. You may say many things before you get to your lead and many things after, throwing your "lead" into the middle of it all. Or you may save your lead for the end. Either way, your lead gets buried under all the other words before and around it. Sure, you say it, but your audience can easily miss it because there's so much to sift through to find it or to even notice it.

Another way you can lose your lead is by forgetting it, which is especially prone to happen when you save it for later during a conversation. Do you ever find that you forget your lead while you are talking and end up finishing a conversation without saying what you most intended to say? On the flip side, do you ever discover that once you remember your lead during a conversation, you interrupt others to share it for fear that you will forget it again?

The way to avoid burying the lead is to think of your lead as your newspaper headline. Headlines come first. The rest, including the story about the headline and the details, comes later. This way, if someone gets nothing else, they get the main point. Start with your headline. Instead of letting your conversational ship go round and round and wherever the wind blows, you'll have an anchor that you and your listener can use to keep it from straying too far. In this way, when you avoid burying the lead, it becomes a guiding light for your attention. As with paraphrasing, this is a skill to reserve for more complicated or lengthy communications, where your listener can easily become lost.

Balancing Listening and Speaking

We've presented skills to practice as a listener and as a speaker. If you play one role, you usually play the other as well, and conversations involve balancing both roles. On what side do you see an imbalance or on what side do others, again and again, point one out? If it's on the listening side, practice Stop, Look, and Listen Mindfully and/or Paraphrasing. If you practice paraphrasing and struggle with it, practice Stop, Look, and Listen Mindfully or, if it applies, Urge Surfing for interruption. These practices will make paraphrasing easier. (Of course, we realize that your ability to paraphrase also depends on the connection and communication skills of your speaker.)

Speaking and listening skills overlap. The skill of paying attention to your audience shares elements with Stop, Look, and Listen Mindfully and Urge Surfing. When you describe your observations (and observations are experiences), you are also practicing being nonjudgmental (a part of listening mindfully). Nonjudgmental descriptions reduce internal distractions. Finally, when you stop burying the lead, you can become better at noticing others' leads and paraphrasing them.

In this last section on storytelling, we target public speaking. As Greg does, many with ADHD may gravitate toward public speaking when given the chance to share ideas through speech.

Artful Mastery: Storytelling

Perhaps you'll want to practice one other skill as a speaker, especially if you speak publicly by giving presentations, teaching groups, or leading meetings. With a wandering mind, wandering speech often follows. So even if you stop burying the lead, you may lose your audience because you lose the actual story that your lead promises.

Stories have a beginning, middle, and end and our brains, as Dr. Zak (2013) notes, love them. Stories change our brains and are effective ways to communicate experiences and values. Dr. Zak's research shows that the more emotionally engaging the stories, the more they engross our brains and the better we remember them. Two elements define highly engaging stories: (1) they capture and keep our attention and (2) they carry us into the characters' world.

To communicate your experiences and sustain both your attention and your audience's, use what you know about stories that engage you. Effective stories, seen, read, or heard, follow a pattern. We need to know why we are watching or hearing them and what we are meant to learn. Otherwise, according to the research, we tune out. You, as speaker, lose your way. To listen to a string of "we walked to the first bus stop and we walked to the second bus stop and then to the third one," your audience needs to know why these things happened and what you want them to get out of knowing they happened. Pause to ensure that you know the answers to these questions before you share experiences and ideas, particularly when presenting, preaching, and teaching.

Now, if you really want to engage a *large* audience and the stakes are high, watch or listen to the masters. You can check out TED Talks or NPR shows, watch movies, and read or listen to books by master storytellers, such as Mark Twain or Stephen King (we hope we're catching a wide audience here). You can turn to movies by Walt Disney and notice how Oprah Winfrey ran her talk shows. Some scholars assert, with research backing them up, that engaging stories have an "arc." First, something interesting, novel, and maybe even unexpected happens (a dinosaur's created using the DNA of different dinosaurs). Next, tension builds as the characters face obstacles that they must overcome, whether these are external, internal, or both (the dinosaur escapes and turns out to be deadly). The tension leads to a climax where the characters achieve a discovery, fulfill their quest, and transform because of it, leading to resolution (most of those foolish enough to meddle with nature die as punishment while those wise enough to recognize the error of the meddling survive, learning from the journey to survival). Can you recognize *Jurassic World*? The next time you watch a movie that engages you, notice its arc.

If you struggle with storytelling through words, use visuals. Pictures, drawings, and videos are all effective ways to communicate. How many visuals have moved you emotionally, convinced you intellectually, or lingered with you obstinately?

Key Points from Chapter 5

- Several skills come into play when we communicate and connect to one another.

- Use *Know Thyself 5* to identify how you communicate and connect with others, or how you miscommunicate and misconnect.

- Use the *Challenge Thyself 5* practices to increase skills as listener, speaker, or both, and to practice specific skills within each area.

CHAPTER 6

Overcoming Obstacles

During a workshop she attended, Tonya accepted a mission handed down to all attendees: do something pleasant before the next day. So after the workshop, she got on her rented bike and headed to a used bookstore she'd read about. As she rode, she discovered that a Cape Cod summer day was the wrong time for biking with jeans. Still, she rode. When the unshaded path turned uphill and stayed that way for turn after turn, her heart began to sink. Still, she rode. Hot, tired, and with jeans sticking to her, she pulled over to find out how close she was to her destination. On the map, it had seemed close enough for her to have arrived after an hour of riding. As it turned out, she still had another hour to go. This was her turning point. She headed back home, relieved for the downhill start of her return. The next day, the leader of the workshop asked if someone who'd had any difficulties with the assigned home practice would come up. Tonya did. At the front of a room of hundreds, she told the leader about how her intended pleasant event had turned unpleasant. The workshop leader replied, "That happens." As intended, this gave Tonya pause. Then it stuck.

Obstacles are part of life. We have somewhere to be and there's traffic. We need to get home for the holidays and our flight's canceled. A deadline comes for an unfinished task and we get sick. We buy a sink from IKEA and their pipe sizes and positions are nonstandard, so we are unable to fit them into the bathroom wall as planned. We set out to a destination without knowing how far it really is and what we really need to reach it. Obstacles happen. We need to know how to respond to them to get what we want out of the circumstances, even if it's second best. Tantrums and giving up are unlikely to get us what we ultimately want. In this chapter, we present obstacles to starting and sustaining skills practice and to other areas of your life, along with solutions.

Let's start with a little review. We have shared ways for you to bend your brain biases to your will. We started with turning up the dopamine for essential low-interest areas of your life by combining them with what's of high interest to you. Then we practiced pulling the future into the present by tying it to immediate gratification (carrot) or immediate threat (stick). From there, we worked to engineer your environment to externalize attention and action regulation functions. Subsequently, we worked to engineer your interior to strengthen these functions internally through daily habits and healthy relationships. All these strategies offer ways that you can create your own interventions, internal and external.

Yet you face a bind. When it comes to changing the things that you want to change, you encounter the same competition for your attention that you had prior to reading this book: the promise of a quick dopamine release. In our immediate gratification-ready world, if you are bored or want relief from the anxiety of starting a task, all you have to do is check out by checking the latest social media posts, playing a game, or reading various sites with the day's news. It's so easy, and it matches your brain's desires for a good moment or day. Sure, it may be at the cost of your brain's desires for a good life—but you can always get to that later, right?

Start Through Play

An immediate gratification world works for the emotional part of your brain: the part that wants to dine out, order dessert, drink at leisure, and then pay for it all on credit. Your emotional brain has a hard time seeing the future clearly, so delayed payment suits it just fine. It's another part of your brain that has a problem with this. Your reasonable brain sees the future and connects your present actions to it. It wants you to think about the wealth and health of your future self. In all our brains, the emotional and reasonable parts compete for attention. In your brain, your more impulsive, impatient emotional brain often wins.

When your emotional brain wins, again and again, its neural connections get stronger, increasing the chance that it will defeat your reasonable brain at the next battle and the next. When a behavior increases your dopamine levels, your emotional brain says, "Let's do it again." What about your reasonable brain? When your emotional and reasonable brain are at odds—your emotional brain says chocolate cake and your reasonable brain says apple—the reasonable brain has to use its powers of reason to defeat the emotional brain at its own game. If you've struggled with putting the practices we've suggested into action, you may need to flip how you see them.

In his book *Drive*, Dan Pink recalls Mark Twain's Tom Sawyer character and the time Tom got his friends to help him whitewash his aunt's fence by convincing them it was a prized privilege. The boys had so much fun whitewashing the fence that afterward Tom had an epiphany about the nature of work and play: work can become play under the right conditions. Dan Pink calls it the Sawyer Effect. As sociologist Christine Carter (2011) points out, the Sawyer Effect captures research findings about how to increase motivation: turn what you do into play. This is also what we've tried to achieve through dopaminizing. In business, it's called playification (Waters 2014).

With playification, or the Sawyer Effect if you prefer, you specifically convert boring, lackluster, or forced work (think about the parts of a job you have to do even though you hate them) into play. It's been done for centuries, and continues to be done. Dr. Gray notes that there's no less "play-like work" than work that is "mind-numbingly repetitive and dull" and describes hunter-gatherer societies' skillful ways of turning such work into play and jovial occasions by, for example, conducting most work socially instead of alone (Gray 2009, 502). Dr. Carter (2011) gives a modern example of kitchen time equating to play time as her family turns emptying the dishwasher into "part dance-party."

If you've been stuck, join the party and try turning your practice of skills into play. One way to do this if you are a party of one is to use stories to *start* and *sustain* your attention and action to a task. Tasks can become quests that you, the hero, must achieve by overcoming obstacles. Storytelling works as one way to turn up the interest level of a task. Perhaps your "quest" is remodeling your house. One of your obstacles may be that you, on this particular quest for the first time, acquire your sink, with its pipes, from IKEA, which has pipes meant to fit into Swedish homes that are nonstandard for American ones. What do you, the hero, do? *The hero, faced with a puzzle of mismatched pieces that she must solve to continue her journey, contemplates her options. She must find her way to and through the maze of the blue-and-gold fortress where she bought the mismatched pieces or seek out the local magician who knows the trick of matching the fortress's parts to the parts of her home.* All heroes have obstacles to overcome.

Start Through Rewarding Effectively

The intrinsic rewards of play can be combined with extrinsic rewards, which also help your reasonable brain to beat your emotional brain at its own game. You may have tried using rewards to dopaminize tasks or as substitutes for more distant future rewards, and concluded that rewards are ineffective. We have seen that this conclusion often results from a few particular mistakes of rewarding.

One common mistake is to mistime rewards. Rewards need to come as soon as possible *after* a desired action and *only* if the desired action occurs. If you are going to give yourself something regardless of whether you follow through with an action, you are separating the action from the reward. The reward then loses its power to influence you. A reward also loses its power if the reward does nothing for you. For example, you may ordinarily find a sweet rewarding, but if you're already satiated when it comes time for your reward of a sweet, it will be less sweet.

Also, repeatedly using the same rewards can deplete their rewarding qualities. Mix it up. Novelty and change trigger dopamine.

Sustain Through Change

You can use novelty and change both to start attention and action and to sustain them. Dr. Gray (2009) describes hunter-gatherer societies as keeping work interesting and engaging by keeping it varied and challenging. Video game developers keep gamers interested through creating various levels to achieve and worlds to explore. Use this knowledge. Remember Dr. Carter's kitchen time turned playtime? Other than dancing while unloading the dishwasher, her children contribute to cooking by inventing their own recipes, with a rule: they are unable to repeat the same meal more than twice during the same month. This keeps them off the road of routine. No avocado macaroni and cheese day after day, please.

If you find that you have a strong start with skills and strategies that diminishes over time, you may need to use them in a different context or try stimulating your senses to make the experience of using them a novel one. Let's look at how this works. In chapter 1, we described dopaminizing bill paying with Facebook by, for example, having Facebook bill-paying buddies keep you on deadline through accountability and cheerleading.

If this worked for a few weeks, and as the novelty faded, you lost interest, you could reengage by changing the context of bill paying by Facebook. Instead of just posting bill-paying activity to your accountability buddies, you could schedule an online meeting—perhaps a Skype session or a FaceTime chat. Or your novel angle could involve your senses. For example, you could light candles of some favorite scents to envelop you as you work on your bill-paying posts. Dr. McGonigal (2013) describes how a lover of Christmas dopaminized a chore she'd been procrastinating by evoking Christmas through music and possibly scents. Imagine Christmas music and candle scents during the summer! Daredevil.

Sustain Through a Response Plan

We've all heard of emergency response plans, where we prepare for emergency situations before they happen. Greg likes response plans for when you feel tempted to stop practicing skills. His response plan owes its inspiration to addiction relapse prevention (Larimer, Palmer, & Marlatt 1999). It involves knowing where you want to be, what will derail you, and what will keep you on track so you can prepare ahead. Time to get out your journal.

KNOW THYSELF 6: Response Planning

To begin this exercise, identify triggers for giving up on strategies and skills. What derails you? These triggers may be internal, such as negative thoughts, or external, such as the end of a relationship or another stressor. Remember triggers related to health, such as becoming sick or having a medical condition flare up. Jot these down into your journal under "Triggers."

Second, identify core skills and habits that you can use daily to counteract the effects of triggers. For each one of your triggers, link the specific counteracting skills and habits you will use. For example, you might counteract the derailing effects of illness through healthy eating, getting enough sleep, and mindfulness practice.

Third, identify resources, including social networks, to keep you on track with skills practice or with particular skills (e.g., an exercise group).

Fourth, schedule a regular time each week to review your triggers to check off any that are present and to put your counteractive measures into practice.

Perhaps you are saying this is all fine and dandy but to get on the skill-sustaining train, you first have to figure out how to get off the train you are on. And the train you are on has such dazzling lights, you are unable to turn away from them. Perhaps you feel hopeless.

Stop and Shift by Exchanging Criticism for Compassion

You may find that you struggle to put down the phone, turn off the TV, and say no to another night out or other activity. Procrastination is immediately gratifying. When you delay having to face something that bores or stresses you, you experience immediate relief, which is powerfully gratifying. It's so gratifying that relief from painful withdrawal keeps addictions going once their pleasure disappears. When you are faced with a stressful project or need to study material that bores you, putting it off by getting online gives you immediately satisfying relief and the promise of excitement. Dopamine jackpot!

Along with this struggle to say no to procrastination, you may criticize and condemn yourself. You may hope to motivate yourself with criticism—with the thought that if you just felt sufficiently disgusted with yourself, you'd change. If self-disgust worked to get you what you really want, our job would be to help pile it on. But criticism, condemnation, and self-disgust only keep you buried.

Greg and Tonya work with many self-punishment masters. They criticize and castigate themselves for procrastinating on working toward a good life or even a good month by choosing a more exciting or less boring *now*. As a result, science suggests, they unwittingly enter into a self-defeating cycle, feeding their procrastination by berating themselves for it. The same unintended feeding of symptoms with criticism may occur between parents and youth with ADHD. Researchers recently found that children with ADHD entering adolescence show a lower chance of symptom decline when they have highly and consistently critical parents, versus parents who express consistently low levels of criticism or both low and high levels of criticism over time (Musser et al. 2016). To stop a self-defeating cycle of criticism and procrastination and shift to what you really want, be kind to yourself. It's never too late.

Self-compassion—being kind to yourself and recognizing your connection to humanity when you are suffering or experience a failure (Neff 2011)—will motivate you. The more of it you have, the more emotional well-being you have, the less anxious you are, and the less you avoid and procrastinate. High procrastinators have less self-compassion than low procrastinators (e.g., Williams, Stark, & Foster 2008). And research shows that when we procrastinate on a task and forgive ourselves, which is related to self-compassion, we are actually *less likely* to procrastinate on the same kind of task the next time it comes around (e.g., Wohl, Pychyl, & Bennett 2010). Mental disengagement appears to appeal to us more when we lack self-compassion, as a study of college students' perceptions of academic failure shows. In the study, students responding to perceived failure with self-compassion were able to stay academically interested and involved, whereas less self-compassionate students showed more avoidance of the reality through mental disengagement (such as excessive sleep and drugs) and denial (Neff, Hsieh, & Dejitterat 2005).

To stop attending to your distractions and shift your attention to where you need it, give yourself what psychotherapist Linda Graham (2014) calls "a self-compassion break." If you become overwhelmed, disappointed, or frustrated and feel tempted to turn to distractions, see what happens if, instead, you turn to self-compassion. The Hand over Heart practice is one way to do this. Another research-based self-compassion practice to consider is a loving-kindness meditation (see text box).

Loving-Kindness Meditation

A meditation to cultivate compassion and positive emotions by wishing others and self well.

Imagine someone you love without reservation (perhaps a child or pet). Imagine this loved one right here with you and mentally send them these wishes:

May you be safe. May you be secure. May you be at ease. May you be free from suffering. May you be happy.

Imagine this loved one turns to you and sends you these same wishes.

Now send these wishes to yourself (or at least their possibility):

May I be safe. May I be secure. May I be at ease. May I be free from suffering. May I be happy.

End with,

May all beings be happy.

Found to increase positive emotions over time, which then build personal resources (increased mindfulness, life purpose, and social support; decreased illness symptoms), which then predict increased life satisfaction and decreased depressive symptoms.

(Fredrickson et al. 2008)

CHALLENGE THYSELF 6: Hand over Heart

Place your right hand over your heart for a few breaths and notice what you feel. Now replace your right hand with your left hand and do the same. You're likely to notice that you feel more when using one hand than when using the other.

Next, stop anything else you are doing and place your higher-feeling hand over your heart. Say something kind to yourself, something you might say to your own suffering child, if you have one, such as, "Oh, my love" or "I know. I'm here." A kind physical gesture such as this one can soothe you at the physiological level (Neff 2011). Do this for three to five minutes. To test its soothing power, count your heartbeats at your wrist or neck for ten seconds before you do the practice and then again for ten seconds after you do it. If you are already very calm, you may notice no difference, so test the effect of the practice when you want to feel calmer and more at peace.

If you want a more exterior way to practice self-compassion, consider a ritual that restores you and connects you to your common humanity. Greg finds self-compassion through labyrinth walks. These walks consist of following a winding path to its center, resting at the center, and, when ready, walking out of the spiral to, once again, face the world. Some find the rituals offered at church increase their self-compassion.

Stop and Shift by Validating

Often with ADHD, you hear, again and again, that you need to change. "You need to stop doing this. You need to start doing that." Change can be hard. And when no one seems to get it or get you, it can be even harder. Sometimes you just need to be truly seen, to feel understood. A hard or painful task becomes a lot easier to face when someone acknowledges the difficulty. If you're struggling with achieving changes that you desire, try validating your struggle.

What Is Validation?

Validating means seeing your thoughts, feelings, and behaviors and acknowledging their legitimacy—the ways in which they are legitimate or make sense. They could make sense because of who you are, where you come from, your current circumstances, or because they are simply normal and how most people would respond. Validation accepts the reasonableness of your thoughts, feelings, and behaviors, without necessarily approving of or agreeing with them. And, according to theory and research, it may pave the way for change. Acceptance opens us to the possibility of change (e.g., of our habits).

Validation may be best remembered through a story. Tonya heard this story from Pastor Jim Black of her girlhood church. Pastor Black loved to tell stories to keep his congregation's attention and this is one that has stayed with her. *A boy was eating out with his parents when the waitress came by and asked him what he wanted. The boy said, "I'll have a hamburger and fries and a chocolate shake." His mother then said, "No, he'll have the chicken with vegetables and a glass of milk." Turning to the boy, the waitress said, "Ketchup with your fries?" When the waitress walked away, the boy said to his parents, "She thinks I'm real."* Validation is about being seen, being heard, and getting the message that you make sense. At least some part of your perspective is understandable, even if others or even you disapprove of this perspective. And even when others disagree with your viewpoint, there's likely some truth, or validity, to it. Validating is the skill of seeing this truth, large or kernel-sized.

WHY VALIDATE?

We all seek to be understood and accepted, even when we need to change to be more effective. We want to hear, "I see you." Research shows that validation soothes us when we're stressed, as shown by various measures, including of physiological arousal (e.g., Shenk & Fruzzetti 2011). When we sense that others see our reality, we feel calmer. Our stress decreases. If no one else sees our reality, and we are able to tell ourselves that we make sense when we legitimately do, we soothe ourselves. When we or others invalidate our valid experiences by rejecting them or suggesting that they are unreal, our stress goes up, we feel worse emotionally, and we may be less likely to change.

In one test of this change piece, researchers gave patients with pain complaints repeated pain tests and either validating or invalidating responses to their pain (Linton et al. 2012). Has someone ever invalidated your pain, physical or emotional, by suggesting you were exaggerating or faking? Ouch, right? You just feel worse. These researchers recognized that pain, because it's so subjective, often elicits invalidating responses. They wanted to see how validation, versus invalidation, affects behavior. So they asked the patients, after validating and invalidating them, to submit to an extra pain test, after an agreed-upon number of these tests. Which group do you think said yes at a higher rate? The validated group of patients. The researchers essentially concluded that if doctors want to be heard, they have to start by listening. (This is an example of how acceptance opens the possibility of change.)

Listen to the unheard parts of yourself and notice whether you invalidate them. See what happens when you give them what they need...your understanding. And notice we said understanding instead of problem solving or scolding.

WHAT TO VALIDATE

To start, you might need to validate that what you want to change may look easy and be hard nonetheless. If exercise and healthy eating, for example, were as easy as they sound, would more than a third of US adults be obese (Centers for Disease Control and Prevention 2015a)? The trick is to validate the valid. For example, if someone gives you an ultimatum of "Change or I'm leaving you," it's valid to feel sad and even angry. It's also normal to want to escape pain and understandable that you want to go get drunk to drown your sorrows. It's likely invalid to then go to a bar to get drunk, if you want to keep the relationship and your self-respect. You may want to give up on skills practice because it's hard. It's normal to want to give up when things are really hard. Sticking with practice, despite challenges, also makes sense if it moves you toward, instead of away from, the people and things that matter to you.

LEVELS OF VALIDATION

Linehan defines six levels of validation, with each higher "dose" of validation requiring more effort and skill than the last (Edmond & Keefe 2015, 216). After sharing descriptions and examples of each level for physical pain, we offer examples of each of these levels of validation for struggles with low attention and action regulation. You can use these various examples as a launching pad for self-validation as well as share them nonjudgmentally and at the right time with family and friends. You may even need to validate family and friends so that they are soothed enough to return validation.

Level of Validation	Description	Example for Pain (Edmond & Keefe 2015, 219)
One: Showing Interest	Pay attention and notice. Show interest, asking questions, looking at the person, and even nodding. No multitasking.	Nodding and making eye contact with someone while they share their experience.
Two: Accurate Reflection	Paraphrase what you've heard to show you were really listening and to check your understanding.	Patient: "Compared with yesterday, I hurt a lot more today." Validation: "So, your pain is worse today."
Three: Express What's Unsaid and Implied	Imagine what someone might feel, think, or want under the circumstances. Notice the implications of what's said or shown nonverbally. (Be open to correction.)	Patient: "[...] I have a pain flare every time I try to do something!" Validation: "It sounds like you're frustrated."
Four: Validation of Sufficient or Understandable Causes	Validate that someone's experience or expectation is understandable given their past experiences or who they are.	Patient: "I need more pain medication." Validation: "It makes sense that you would want to take more pain medication [...] it was helpful before."
Five: Validation as Reasonable Response to Present Situation	Communicate that the experience is reasonable given the current circumstances or what most people would feel, think, or do.	Patient: "[...it's impossible for me] to keep doing this yard work." Validation: "It makes sense that you want to take a break from the yard work[;] it's difficult for you to just keep working till you complete the job when your back pain is getting worse."
Six: Radically Genuine	Respond to someone as deserving of the same respect as you and as an equal as a human being. No condescending. See someone as capable of change.	Patient: "I am so worried because my pain is worse again today." Validation: "Of course a pain flare leads you to feel anxious. In the same situation, I would probably feel that way even with what I know about pain [...]."

Validation Examples for ADHD	Others	Self
Level 1	While someone shares his or her experience, give them eye contact and nod to show you're listening. Put your phone away.	When you are hurting, stop and notice your, say, disappointment instead of distracting from it. Be curious and open to your own experiences.
Level 2	"Things used to be easier for me. Now I seem less organized and more forgetful." *Validation: "Some things seem harder for you now."*	*"Some things seem to be becoming harder for me."*
Level 3	"I have so much to do and I keep being told I need to do more. I'd have to stop sleeping to add exercise to my week." *Validation: "You sound frustrated and overwhelmed."*	"I have so much to do and I keep being told I need to do more. I'd have to stop sleeping to add exercise to my week." *Validation: "I notice I'm feeling frustrated and overwhelmed."*
Level 4	"I feel anxious at work now that I've made a few mistakes." *Validation: "Since losing your last job because of mistakes, you've been anxious about it happening again."*	"I feel anxious at work now that I've made a few mistakes." *Validation: "It makes sense that I'm anxious. I've lost my job before because of mistakes."*

147

Validation Examples for ADHD	Others	Self
Level 5	"My boss criticizes me constantly. I just want to quit." *Validation: "It's normal to want to quit when you feel criticized constantly at work."* (Notice there's no validation of quitting, as this may actually be invalid under the circumstances.)	"My boss criticizes me constantly. I just want to quit." *Validation: "Who likes criticism? It's normal to want to quit when you feel criticized constantly at work."*
Level 6	"I'm afraid my children will struggle, too." *Validation: "It's normal to want the best for your kids. It's part of being a parent."*	"I'm afraid my children will struggle, too." *Validation: "I just want my kids to have the best shot at a good life."*

Follow Your Own Roads

If you practice and practice the skills and strategies of this book and find that you still keep hitting a wall, consider looking at the world around you. Perhaps it's what you need to change. Are you on the right path *for you?* Following well-worn paths may be disadvantageous, particularly when these paths are designed for typical brains.

Tonya has often noticed when driving (and cycling) that most drivers stick to the same roads as other drivers, even when it gets them to places more slowly and with a higher chance of frustration. She will turn off main roads during times of high traffic and almost always find another street a block or two away that's parallel to the main road and practically deserted. It reminds her each time of how prone we are to do what's familiar. Creating a life you find worth living may mean veering off the main paths and finding less traveled roads where your "deficit," "disruption," and "disorder" let you soar. It may be finding what Hallowell (2015) calls your "sweet spot," where you are doing what you love and are good at doing. With your brain, if you are surrounded by repetition and routine at work, school, or home, it's unlikely you've found your sweet spot. Your sweet spot's likely to be atypical.

Even Smoother Roads Will Have Bumps

Once upon a time, we the people of mental health, scholarship, and science believed that children and teens could "recover" from, or mature out of, ADHD. Scientists have uncovered a more complex reality.

In 2014, MIT neuroscientists conducted the first comparison of the brain activity of three groups: adults without ADHD, adults with ADHD (who met criteria as children and as adults), and adults "recovered" from ADHD (who met criteria as children and no longer met criteria as adults) (Mattfield et al.

2014). The researchers focused on two "networks": a do-nothing network called the default mode network and a do-something network called the task-positive network.

In adults without ADHD, all was as expected. First, during rest, the default mode network (the network associated with rest, daydreaming, and doing nothing) appeared active and efficient, with its major brain regions (the posterior cingulate cortex and the medial prefrontal cortex) working together. Second, when the default mode network turned up, the task positive network (the we-have-a-task-to-do network) turned down and vice versa. The two networks each had their turn when it was their time to be active. With ADHD, a different picture surfaced.

In adults with ADHD, first, the two major regions of the default mode network mentioned above (the posterior cingulate cortex and the medial prefrontal cortex) failed to synchronize, or work at the same time and rate. Second, the default mode network and the task positive network both turned up at the same time. When these networks compete instead of cooperate, the ability to focus suffers. Here we see a brain activating you to be focused and unfocused at the same time.

In ADHD-"recovered" adults, the default mode network looked like that of normal adults, with its major regions working together. But their default mode and task positive networks showed simultaneous activity just as they did for adults with ADHD.

Both ADHD groups (recovered and persistent ADHD) performed poorly on tests of executive function compared with the normal group. In some ways, then, it appears that ADHD can be undone for certain people...but only partly. This study was the first to show that ADHD leaves its mark on your brain's patterns of activity. Scientists just needed to know where to look.

With ADHD appearing to be a forever disorder, you are likely to confront your brain differences, again and again. Your brain has real differences from the par-for-the-course brain. What you accept and what you try to change both inside and outside is ultimately up to you. We hope you will use your differences to your advantage as much as possible.

This talk about using your differences likely brings up two questions that we want to answer for you before ending this book: How does medication fit into using your differences when the purpose of medication is to decrease them? What desired differences, or gifts, does ADHD bring you?

What About Medications?

Our ADHD group members often come with questions about medications and, from scouring the literature and consulting with our prescribing colleagues, we've learned that the answers are somewhat complicated. On the one hand, trusted sources on ADHD Russell Barkley and Thomas E. Brown point to extensive research showing that, for most individuals with ADHD, ADHD medications significantly reduce symptoms when used as prescribed. On the other hand, a recent review of 44 studies involving almost 10,000 adults with ADHD indicates that this reduction may decrease over time and, for most, comes with unwanted side effects (Cunill et al. 2016). These side effects and other complications for older adults (aged 65 and up) may increase the known risks to a level that outweighs observed benefits (Goodman et al. 2016; Torgersen et al. 2016). Beyond known side effects, big or small, there's still a lot that's unknown about the brain, including how the persistent use of anti-ADHD drugs over a long period affects it. And some scholars, such as Caltech professor David Anderson, PhD, raise questions about whether the nonspecific way these drugs work makes sense and how much this matters.

In his 2013 Ted Talk about ADHD, Dr. Anderson discusses how the drugs used for complex psychiatric disorders globally increase levels of a neurotransmitter, such as dopamine, though only specific neural circuits appear to need it. He says this is like pouring oil all over the engine of a car so that some of it trickles to the low-oil parts, with "a lot of it doing more harm than good" (Anderson 2013). Scientists are trying to identify how drugs can target delivery to specific neurons and brain regions, rather than simply increasing the levels of neurotransmitters globally, as if the brain were "a bag of chemicals" (Anderson 2013). The hope is that this will create desired changes without undesired side effects.

Given the complexity involved with medicating a multifaceted condition, we are unable to answer many of our members' questions to their satisfaction. Generally, these questions boil down to one: Will medication be of more help to me than harm? With all that's unknown, we leave members to evaluate whether medication proves more helpful or harmful to them and how comfortable they are with uncertainty.

What About Gifts?

It's normal to ask about gifts, strengths, talents, or advantages associated with disorders. Although you can go online and find books about ADHD bestowing gifts of leadership, creativity, athleticism, and more, you may be asking what we have to say about them.

We, too, started off asking these questions. The stakes are high for us, too. Greg has ADHD. Tonya's husband and oldest child have it and whether her toddler later ends up diagnosed with it remains to be seen. We felt our hearts leap at the reassurance of the gifts we mentioned above, such as leadership. Eager to share the abundant research showing evidence of these abilities, we searched the books and sites proclaiming these gifts to find their sources. We found that, if they cited anything, they cited other books about these gifts, which cited other books. The original research eluded us. Given her research background, Tonya combed through research databases, again and again, hoping to find more than she found. But she came up nearly empty. The research fails to offer evidence that ADHD bestows any of the widely proclaimed gifts on adults and adolescents, with the exception of three studies. At the same time, studying creativity has hardly been on scientists' agenda...until recently. So there's still much to learn.

Three studies show increased original creative thinking, also known as divergent thinking, associated with post-childhood ADHD. Divergent thinking is more popularly known as the ability to "think out of the box." A German study on adolescents showed that teens with, versus without, ADHD, when asked to invent novel things, invented more original and less practical objects (Abraham et al. 2006). They were unusual, unusable inventions. In the United States, researchers found similar results looking at adults. Undergraduate college students with ADHD scored higher on divergent thinking and lower on convergent thinking than students without ADHD (White & Shah 2006). They were better at coming up with unusual uses for common household objects but worse at identifying a word related to three other words. In the third study, researchers found that college students with ADHD showed higher levels of creative thinking on a verbal task and reported higher levels of real-world creative achievement than did students without ADHD (White & Shah 2011). In this same sample of college students, those with ADHD preferred coming up with ideas, whereas those without ADHD preferred clarifying and developing ideas.

At the same time, there's research suggesting no reliable connection between ADHD symptoms and divergent thinking (Zabelina, Condon, & Beeman 2014), and a review of 72 experiments on creativity and brain activity found no special association between creative thinking and defocused attention (Dietrich & Kanso 2010).

Creativity appears to be a perplexing puzzle of many pieces. It's associated with several different personality dimensions and, brain-wise, turns out to be quite complex. One of the personality dimensions associated with both creativity and ADHD appears to be low conscientiousness (Feist 1998; Gomez & Corr 2014), which includes being disorganized, spontaneous, and careless versus organized, self-disciplined, and thorough (McCrae & Costa 1987). But creativity goes along with more than low conscientiousness. It also involves more than one area of the brain. Although scientists know relatively little about the brain components of creativity and have only recently begun to study them (Wiggins & Bhattacharya 2014), so far studies show that creativity extends beyond a few particular brain regions. And, contrary to popular ideas, creativity involves both the right and left cerebral hemispheres.

When asked about the gifts of ADHD, here's what Tonya now tells her group members: "There's no need to look to ADHD for your gifts. You can have gifts with or without ADHD." And when she sees the gifts of her husband and son, she remembers this. They and you are more than your ADHD. Sometimes you and others around you may forget this. And, really, a general link or no link between ADHD and creativity really tells you nothing specific about *you*.

In Conclusion

This book is about you. Try all the skills and strategies it offers—dopaminizing, mindfulness, guiding and flashing lights, cues, and so on—to move closer to the life you really want to be living instead of away from it. Remember the questions the Amish ask? Here's a question to guide you: Does the practice of the skills here move you toward or away from who and what you really care about? If they move you toward these things, we ask that you give all the skills a fair chance, and your best effort. Who and what you care about are the desired direction on your compass. We are confident that many of the skills and strategies we've shared will move you there.

Key Points from Chapter 6

- Obstacles are part of the path rather than deviations from it. Be ready for them. You can overcome many of them.

- Start your attention and action through play and effective rewarding.

- Sustain your attention and action through change and a response plan.

- Stop and shift through compassion and validation.

- Above all, use the strategies and skills here to move mostly toward rather than away from who and what you really care about.

Acknowledgments

In more than one way, ADHD shaped the creation of this book. After Greg retired from Kaiser Permanente, he continued mentoring Tonya, who began running the ADHD groups he had started. They'd been meeting regularly at Barnes & Noble for months when Greg told Tonya he had a chance to write a book. He'd been presenting on ADHD all over the nation and New Harbinger Publications noticed. Greg said he was thinking of declining the offer. His communication talents landed on speaking. With his ADHD and dyslexia, he'd always struggled with writing. Tonya told him he had to find a way to get words on paper, such as by recording his talks and then having someone transcribe them. Over a year later, Greg had put to paper only initial, albeit big, ideas for the book. As he and Tonya discussed these ideas, he asked Tonya to collaborate with him. Thus, this book came into being, with Greg and Tonya sharing big ideas and Tonya then putting them down on paper, turning two voices into one.

For allowing the creation of this book, we'd like to thank our families, first and foremost. When you have a family, they sacrifice to give you time to think, read, research, and write. They listen to your ideas and share their thoughts, giving suggestions about what to keep, what to cut, and what to change. Sometimes they even add images and jokes about you or them to your text. Greg thanks his wife Jackie for her encouraging and pragmatic help as well as her dry sense of humor when responding to some of his ideas. She keeps their discussions engaging and entertaining. Tonya thanks her husband Sergio for reading the *entire* book and giving feedback, including rereading chapters more than once. (He'd like to add that he read the entire book three times to give feedback.) Tonya also thanks her son for wanting to read the entire book…until he saw how many pages it was. And she thanks both her husband and son for offering up examples of their own experiences with low attention and action regulation.

We'd like to thank some other individuals and groups as well. We both are grateful for what we've learned from our work as mental health therapists about low attention and action regulation and about the individuals who have it. And we thank the editors at New Harbinger Publications who asked for this book and shaped it, including Vicraj Gill, who advised us all along the way, rewrite after rewrite. Tonya's grateful that Greg asked her to join him on this journey, and Greg appreciates Tonya's willingness to collaborate and give birth to this book.

Greg also thanks Lauretta Young, MD, for her encouragement and support during the early 1990s when Greg wanted to introduce ADHD groups to Kaiser Permanente's Northwest clinics. And he thanks Mike Long, LCSW, JD, the attorney for the Oregon Attorney Assistance Program, for his 2012 vision of statewide services to lawyers with ADHD. He would also like to thank his fellow therapist buddies Donald Altman, LPC, and John Kuzma, LCSW, for their support and encouragement.

Tonya thanks Bill Soles, LPC, her supervisor at Kaiser Permanente, for allowing her to run ADHD groups instead of sticking to the "core" ones.

APPENDIX A

Resources

Apps

For paced breathing:

BreathPacer, https://itunes.apple.com/us/app/breathpacer/
id291943364?mt=8

To block Internet distractions:

Freedom at https://www.freedom.to (for PC) or
SelfControl at http://www.selfcontrolapp.com (for Mac)

To stay on task: StayOnTask at

https://play.google.com/store/apps/details?id=valavg.
stayontask&hl=en

StayOnTask offers a tone at random intervals. The tone is your cue to stop and check whether you're on task. When you're on task, you have a chance to reward yourself. If you are off task, you have a chance to reroute.

Online Resources

If you'd like to learn about, and even join, a community that invites connection and offers resources and events for individuals with low attention and action regulation:

http://www.add.org

For the latest and greatest developments on ADHD as well as video clips and articles:

http://www.russellbarkley.org

http://www.drthomasebrown.com

For commitment contracts: StickK at

http://www.stickk.com

The website lets you practice precommitment through contracts, public or private, to achieve your goals. You can put money on the line to go to a charity you like or one you dislike (an anti-charity) if you fail to achieve your goals, as determined by your designated "referee."

Physical and Mental Health

For Belly Breathing instructions with visuals:

https://myhealth.alberta.ca/health/pages/conditions.aspx?hwId=aa141579

For weekly self-care logs or diaries (including for nutrition and exercise):

http://www.depressiontoolkit.org/toolsandchecklists

For sleep:

> http://www.depressiontoolkit.org/download/2-weeksleep
> diary.pdf

> https://www.sleepfoundation.org/sleep-diary/SleepDiaryv6.
> pdf

Physical Activity Guidelines:

> www.cdc.gov/physicalactivity/basics/adults/

Prioritizing

These websites break down the elements of prioritizing. Four boxes defined by urgency and importance show which of your activities require your attention first and which last. Both sites below offer a range of examples of how to use these magical four boxes:

> http://www.artofmanliness.com/2013/10/23/
> eisenhower-decision-matrix

> http://www.sidsavara.com/personal-development/
> nerdy-productivity-coveys-time-management-matrix-
> illustrated-with-xkcd-comics

Interpersonal Neurobiology

Learn about interpersonal neurobiology and find therapists who apply it as well as resources on it at

> http://www.mindgains.org/resources

Mindfulness Resources

Guided mindfulness instructions and meditations at

> https://www.calm.com (for download to your phone)

> http://www.marc.ucla.edu (English and Spanish meditations for listening or downloading to iTunes)

Loving-kindness resource:

> http://www.greatergood.berkeley.edu/raising_happiness/post/better_than_sex_and_appropriate_for_kids

Mindful eating tip sheet available at

> https://www.uhs.berkeley.edu/eda/7Mindful.pdf

Mindful eating resources, including research on mindless eating and the effects of cues, free visual cues, printable worksheets, and guidance on what works:

> http://www.mindlesseating.org

Overview of Diagnostic Criteria for Adult ADHD

An enduring pattern of inattention and/or hyperactivity-impulsivity that disrupts development or functioning across settings. This disruption appears, for adults, through at least five symptoms of (1) and/or at least five symptoms of (2) below. The symptoms must be demonstrated often and have been present prior to age 12.

1. Inattention

   a. Overlooks details or makes careless mistakes (e.g., work is inaccurate).

   b. Has difficulty staying focused during tasks/activities such as lectures.

   c. Seems to wander mentally when spoken to directly.

   d. Lacks follow-through on instructions and fails to finish work, chores, and duties.

   e. Has difficulty organizing tasks (e.g., poor time management; messy work).

   f. Avoids and resists tasks demanding sustained effort (e.g., preparing reports).

g. Loses necessary things (e.g., wallets, keys, eyeglasses, mobile phones).

h. Easily distracted including by thoughts unrelated to what's at hand.

i. Daily living forgetfulness (e.g., chores and errands; paying bills, returning calls).

2. Hyperactivity and impulsivity

a. Fidgets, taps, or squirms.

b. Leaves seat when this is unexpected (e.g., during class or work meeting).

c. Feels and/or shows restlessness.

d. Unable to play or recreate quietly.

e. Seems to be "on the go" (e.g., unable to be still for long periods).

f. Talks excessively.

g. Blurts out answers before question finished (e.g., finishes others' sentences).

h. Difficulty waiting for a turn (e.g., when gets into a line).

i. Interrupts or intrudes on others (e.g., takes over what others are doing).

Source: American Psychiatric Association. 2013. *Diagnostic and Statistical Manual of Mental Disorders, 5th Edition.* Arlington, VA: American Psychiatric Publishing.

Recommendations for Engineering Work, School, and Home Environments to Regulate Attention and Action

- Look at where a schedule, project, class, or job change could let you do things that are more stimulating and interesting to you. For example, could you insert some physicality into an activity? When Tonya watches instructional therapy videos, she jogs.

- Reduce distractions by closing doors, moving away from high-traffic areas (e.g., a room where many pass by or through), and moving an inbox outside your office for deliveries.

- Have visible and external reminders of what you need to do, including instructions and deadlines. Phrases that stick with you also help. If you start things without finishing them, a useful phrase may be "Beginnings have endings." This also works with remembering daily things around your home, such as closing doors you've opened, turning off lights you've turned on, etc.

- Break tasks down into chunks to avoid overfocusing, set a time to stop, and use an attention-getting alarm to alert you when you've reached your allotted time.

- Immediately, frequently reward yourself when you regulate your attention and action.

- Keep your rewards fresh and exciting, with several reward options.

- If you do a lot of sitting, give yourself several short breaks during the day to move around, even if it's just to walk around the block.

- Use your planner to write down what you need to remember from conversations with a boss, professor, etc., rather than relying on memory (e.g., that you said you'd send a particular e-mail).

- If you are chronically late, aim to arrive early instead of on time.

- Before you commit to something, review your current commitments and how far you've come on them. See when you have set aside time for these commitments and whether there's room for another one, given your need to eat, sleep, and exercise, among other things.

- Consider recording work/study habits to learn more about where your attention and action go.

Sources: Barkley (2008) and Carnes & Holloway (2009).

References

Abraham, A., S. Windmann, R. Siefen, I. Daum, and O. Güntürkün. 2006. "Creative Thinking in Adolescents with Attention Deficit Hyperactivity Disorder (ADHD)." *Child Neuropsychology* 12(2): 111–123.

Aguirre Castaneda, R. L., S. M. Kumar, R. G. Voigt, C. L. Leibson, W. J. Barbaresi, A. L. Weaver, J. M. Killian, and S. K. Katusic. 2016. "Childhood Attention-Deficit/Hyperactivity Disorder, Sex, and Obesity." *Mayo Clinic Proceedings* 91(3): 352–361.

American Psychological Association. 2006. "Multitasking: Switching Costs." Retrieved from http://www.apa.org/research /action/multitask.aspx.

American Psychiatric Association. 2013. *Diagnostic and Statistical Manual of Mental Disorders, 5th Edition.* Arlington, VA: American Psychiatric Publishing.

Anderson, D. 2013, January 18. "Drugs, Dopamine and Drosophila—A Fly Model for ADHD?" [Video file]. Retrieved from http://www.tedxcaltech.com/content/david-anderson.

Ariely, D. 2011. "Self Control: The Problem and How to Get Over It." [Video file]. Retrieved from http://tedxtalks.ted .com/video/TEDx-Duke-Dan-Ariely-on-Self-Co.

Baird, A. L., A. N. Coogan, A. Siddiqui, R. M. Donev, and J. Thome. 2012. "Adult Attention-Deficit Hyperactivity Disorder Is Associated with Alterations in Circadian Rhythms at the Behavioural, Endocrine and Molecular Levels." *Molecular Psychiatry* 17(10): 988–995.

Baek, R. 2013. "Apps Block Social Media Because Users Can't Help Themselves." Retrieved 16 July 2016 from http://www .npr.org/sections/alltechconsidered/2013/07/23/204848805 /distractions-in-the-digital-age-call-for-apps-to-block-sites.

Barkley, R. 2008. "Classroom Accommodations for Children with ADHD." *The ADHD Report*. Retrieved from http:// www.russellbarkley.org/factsheets/ADHD_School _Accommodations.pdf.

Barkley, R. 2012. *Executive Functions: What They Are, How They Work, and Why They Evolved*. New York, NY: Guilford Press.

Barkley, R. 2014. "Sluggish Cognitive Tempo (Concentration Deficit Disorder?): Current Status, Future Directions, and a Plea to Change the Name." *Journal of Abnormal Child Psychology* 42(1): 117–125.

Barkley, R. 2016. "Commentary: One Way Attention-Deficit/ Hyperactivity Disorder Can Be Life Threatening? A Travelogue on Nikolas et al. (2016)." *Journal of Child Psychology and Psychiatry* 57(2): 149–151.

Belenky, G., N. J. Wesensten, D. R. Thorne, M. L. Thomas, H. C. Sing, D. P. Redmond, M. B. Russo, and T. J. Balkin. 2003. "Patterns of Performance Degradation and Restoration During Sleep Restriction and Subsequent Recovery: A Sleep Dose-Response Study." *Journal of Sleep Research* 12(1): 1–12.

Bell, J. T., and T. D. Spector. 2011. "A Twin Approach to Unraveling Epigenetics." *Trends in Genetics* 27(3): 116–125.

Benjamin, L. S. 2015. "Every Psychopathology Is a Gift of Love (1993)." In *Visions in Psychotherapy Research and Practice: Reflections from the Presidents of the Society for Psychotherapy Research*, edited by Bernhard M. Strauss, Jacques P. Barber, and Louis G. Castonguay. New York, NY: Taylor & Francis.

Bergin, C., and D. Bergin. 2009. "Attachment in the Classroom." *Educational Psychology Review* 21(2): 141–170.

Bertin, M. 2015. "Mindful Eating, ADHD and Nutrition: Poor Eating Habits, Eating Disorders and Being Overweight All May Relate to ADHD." *Psychology Today*, May 12. Retrieved from https://www.psychologytoday.com/blog/child-develop ment-central/201505/mindful-eating-adhd-and-nutrition.

Black, D. W., M. Shaw, B. McCormick, J. D. Bayless, and J. Allen. 2012. "Neuropsychological Performance, Impulsivity, ADHD Symptoms, and Novelty Seeking in Compulsive Buying Disorder." *Psychiatry Research* 200(2–3): 581–587.

Bloch, M. H., and A. Qawasmi. 2011. "Omega-3 Fatty Acid Supplementation for the Treatment of Children with Attention-Deficit/Hyperactivity Disorder Symptomatology: Systematic Review and Meta-analysis." *Journal of the American Academy of Child and Adolescent Psychiatry* 50(10): 991–1000.

Bradt, S. 2004. "Brain Takes Itself on Over Immediate vs. Delayed Gratification: Research May Lead to Advances in Addiction Theory." *Harvard Gazette Archives*, October 21. Retrieved from http://news.harvard.edu/gazette/2004/10.21/07-brain battle.html.

Brady, J. 2013. "Amish Community Not Anti-Technology, Just More Thoughtful." Retrieved from http://www.npr.org /sections/alltechconsidered/2013/09/02/217287028/amish -community-not-anti-technology-just-more-thoughtful.

The Brain Bank North West. 2014. "The Science of Procrastination." Retrieved from http://thebrainbank.scienceblog.com /2014/05/13/the-science-of-procrastination/.

Brown, T. E. 2008. "Executive: Describing Six Aspects of a Complex Syndrome." Retrieved from http://www.drthomasebrown .com/pdfs/Executive_Functions_by_Thomas_Brown.pdf.

Brown, T. E. 2013. *A New Understanding of ADHD in Children and Adults: Executive Function Impairments.* New York, NY: Taylor & Francis.

Carnes, B., and M. Holloway. 2009. "Attention Deficit Hyper-activity Disorder (ADHD) in the Workplace: How to Opti-mize the Performance of Employees with Adult ADHD." *Graziado Business Review* 12(2). Retrieved from https://gbr .pepperdine.edu/2010/08/attention-deficit-hyperactivity -disorder-adhd-in-the-workplace/.

Carter, C. 2011. "Motivated to Do the Dishes." Retrieved from http://greatergood.berkeley.edu/raising_happiness/post/like _chores.

Caye, A., T. B. Rocha, L. Anselmi, J. Murray, A. M. Menezes, F. C. Barros, et al. 2016. "Attention-Deficit/Hyperactivity Dis-order Trajectories from Childhood to Young Adulthood: Evi-dence from a Birth Cohort Supporting a Late-onset Syndrome." JAMA *Psychiatry*, May 18. doi: 10.1001/jama psychiatry.2016.0383.

Cedernaes, J., M. E. Osler, S. Voisin, J. E. Broman, H. Vogel, S. L. Dickson, J. R. Zierath, H. B. Schiöth, and C. Benedict. 2015. "Acute Sleep Loss Induces Tissue-Specific Epigenetic and Transcriptional Alterations to Circadian Clock Genes in Men." *Journal of Clinical Endocrinology & Metabolism* 100(9): E1255-E1261.

Center on the Developing Child at Harvard University. 2015. "Gene-Environment Interaction." Retrieved from http:// developingchild.harvard.edu/science/deep-dives/gene -environment-interaction/.

Centers for Disease Control and Prevention. 2015a. "Adult Obe-sity Facts." Retrieved from http://www.cdc.gov/obesity/data /adult.html.

Centers for Disease Control and Prevention. 2015b. "How Much Physical Activity Do Adults Need?" Retrieved from http:// www.cdc.gov/physicalactivity/basics/adults/.

Centers for Disease Control and Prevention. 2016. "Facts About ADHD." Retrieved from http://www.cdc.gov/ncbddd/adhd /facts.html.

Chandon, P., and B. Wansink. 2012. "Does Food Marketing Need to Make Us Fat? A Review and Solutions." *Nutrition Reviews* 70(10): 571–593.

Chavis, J. M., and M. A. Kisley. 2012. "Adult Attachment and Motivated Attention to Social Images: Attachment-Based Differences in Event-Related Brain Potentials to Emotional Images." *Journal of Research in Personality,* 46(1): 55–62.

Christakis, D. A. 2016. "Rethinking Attention-Deficit/Hyper-activity Disorder." *JAMA Pediatrics* 170(2): 109–110.

Clapp, W. C., M. T. Rubens, J. Sabharwal, and A. Gazzaley. 2011. "Deficit in Switching Between Functional Brain Networks Underlies the Impact of Multitasking on Working Memory in Older Adults." *Proceedings of the National Academy of Sciences* 108(17): 7212–7217.

Commodari, E. (2013). "Preschool Teacher Attachment and Attention Skills." *SpringerPlus* 2: 673. http://doi.org/10.1186 /2193–1801-2-673.

Consumer Reports. 2016. "Get More ZZZs Naturally." February 2016, 81(2): 30.

Coogan, A. N., A. L. Baird, A. Popa-Wagner, and J. Thome. 2016. "Circadian Rhythms and Attention Deficit Hyperactivity Disorder: The What, the When and the Why." *Progress in Neuro-Psychopharmacology and Biological Psychology* 67(3): 74–81.

Cozolino, L. 2013. *The Social Neuroscience of Education: Optimizing Attachment & Learning in the Classroom.* New York, NY: W. W. Norton & Company, Inc.

Cunill, R., X. Castells, A. Tobias, and D. Capellà. 2016. "Efficacy, Safety and Variability in Pharmacotherapy for Adults with Attention Deficit Hyperactivity Disorder: A Meta-analysis and Meta-regression in Over 9000 Patients." *Psychopharmacology* 233(2): 187–197.

Darling-Hammond, L. 2010. *Performance Counts: Assessment Systems that Support High-Quality Learning.* Washington, DC: Council of Chief State School Officers.

Denham, J., F. Z. Marques, B. J. O'Brien, and F. J. Charchar. 2014. "Exercise: Putting Action into Our Epigenome." *Sports Medicine* 44(2): 189–209.

Denton, W. H., B. R. Burleson, T. E. Clark, C. P. Rodriguez, and B. V. Hobbs. 2000. "A Randomized Trial of Emotion-Focused Therapy for Couples in a Training Clinic." *Journal of Marital & Family Therapy* 26(1): 65–78.

Dewitte, M., J. De Houwer, E. H. Koster, and A. Buysse. 2007. "What's in a Name? Attachment-Related Attentional Bias." *Emotion* 7(3): 535–545.

Dietrich, A., and R. Kanso. 2010. "A Review of EEG, ERP, and Neuroimaging Studies of Creativity and Insight." *Psychological Bulletin* 136(5): 822–848.

Division of Sleep Medicine at Harvard Medical School. 2008. "Assess Your Sleep Needs." Retrieved from http://healthysleep.med.harvard.edu/need-sleep/what-can-you-do/assess-needs.

Donfrancesco, R., M. Di Trani, M. C. Porfirio, G. Giana, S. Miano, and E. Andriola. 2015. "Might the Temperament Be a Bias in Clinical Study on Attention-Deficit Hyperactivity Disorder (ADHD)?: Novelty Seeking Dimension as a Core Feature of ADHD." *Psychiatry Research* 227(2–3): 333–338.

Edelstein, R. S. 2006. "Attachment and Emotional Memory: Investigating the Source and Extent of Avoidant Memory Deficits." *Emotion* 6: 340–345.

Edmond, S. N., and F. J. Keefe. 2015. "Validating Pain Communication: Current State of the Science." *Pain* 156(2): 215–219.

Eisenberg, D. T. A., B. Campbell, P. B. Gray, and M. D. Sorenson. 2008. "Dopamine Receptor Genetic Polymorphisms and Body Composition in Undernourished Pastoralists: An Exploration of Nutrition Indices Among Nomadic and

Recently Settled Ariaal Men of Northern Kenya." *BMC Evolutionary Biology* 8(1): 173.

Feist, G. J. 1998. "A Meta-analysis of Personality in Scientific and Artistic Creativity." *Personality and Social Psychology Review* 2(4): 290–309.

Fischman, S., D. P. Kuffler, and C. Bloch. 2015. "Disordered Sleep as a Cause of Attention Deficit/Hyperactivity Disorder: Recognition and Management." *Clinical Pediatrics* 54(8): 713–722.

Flook, L., S. L. Smalley, M. J. Kitil, B. M. Galla, S. Kaiser-Greenland, J. Locke, et al. 2010. "Effects of Mindful Awareness Practices on Executive Functions in Elementary School Children." *Journal of Applied School Psychology* 26: 70–95.

Fraley, C., M. E. Heffernan, A. M. Vicary, and C. C. Brumbaugh. 2011. "The Experiences in Close Relationships—Relationship Structures Questionnaire: A Method for Assessing Attachment Orientations Across Relationships." *Psychological Assessment* 23(3): 615–625.

Fraunberger, E. A., G. Scola, V. L. M. Laliberté, A. Duong, and A. C. Andreazza. 2016. "Redox Modulations, Antioxidants, and Neuropsychiatric Disorders." *Oxidative Medicine and Cellular Longevity* 2016: 1–14

Fredrickson, B. L., M. A. Cohn, K. A. Coffey, J. Pek, and S. M. Finkel. 2008. "Open Hearts Build Lives: Positive Emotions, Induced through Loving-kindness Meditation, Build Consequential Personal Resources." *Journal of Personality and Social Psychology* 95(5): 1045–1062.

Fritz, K. M., and P. J. O'Connor. 2016. "Acute Exercise Improves Mood and Motivation in Young Men with ADHD Symptoms." *Medicine and Science in Sports and Exercise.*

FRONTLINE. 2001. Interview with Russell Barkley. "Medicating Kids." Retrieved from http://www.pbs.org/wgbh/pages/front line/shows/medicating/interviews/barkley.html.

Goel, N., H. Rao, J. S. Durmer, and D. F. Dinges. 2009. "Neuro-cognitive Consequences of Sleep Deprivation." *Seminars in Neurology* 29(4): 320–339.

Gold, M. S., K. Blum, M. Oscar-Berman, and E. R. Braverman. 2014. "Low Dopamine Function in Attention Deficit/Hyperactivity Disorder: Should Genotyping Signify Early Diagnosis in Children?" *Postgraduate Medicine* 126(1): 153–77.

Gomez, R., and P. J. Corr. 2014. "ADHD and Personality: A Meta-analytic Review." *Clinical Psychology Review* 34(5): 376–388.

Gómez-Pinilla, F. 2008. "Brain Foods: The Effects of Nutrients on Brain Function." *Nature Reviews Neuroscience* 9(7): 568–578.

Goodman, D. W., S. Mitchell, L. Rhodewalt, and C. B. Surman. 2016. "Clinical Presentation, Diagnosis and Treatment of Attention-Deficit Hyperactivity Disorder (ADHD) in Older Adults: A Review of the Evidence and Its Implications for Clinical Care." *Drugs & Aging* 33(1): 27–36.

Gorlick, A. 2009. "Media Multitaskers Pay Mental Price, Stanford Study Shows." *Stanford Report*, August 24, 2009. Retrieved from http://news.stanford.edu/news/2009/august24/multitask-research-study-082409.html.

Gotink R. A., P. Chu, J. J. Busschbach, H. Benson, G. L. Friocchione, and M. G. Hunink. 2015. "Standardized Mindfulness-based Interventions in Healthcare: An Overview of Systematic Reviews and Meta-analyses of RCTs." *PLoS One* 10(4):e0124344.

Graham, L. 2014. "Can Self-Compassion Overcome Procrastination?" Retrieved from http://greatergood.berkeley.edu/article/item/can_self_compassion_overcome_procrastination.

Gray, P. 2009. "Play as a Foundation for Hunter-Gatherer Social Existence." *American Journal of Play* 1(4): 476–522.

Hallowell, E. M. 2015. *Driven to Distraction at Work: How to Focus and Be More Productive.* Boston, MA: Harvard Business Review Press.

Hallowell, E. M., and J. J. Ratey. 2005. *Delivered from Distraction: Getting the Most out of Life with Attention Deficit Disorder.* New York, NY: Ballantine.

Hanson, R. 2015. "Just One Thing: Pay Attention!" Retrieved from http://greatergood.berkeley.edu/author/rick_hanson.

Hattie, J. (2011). *Visible Learning for Teachers: Maximizing Impact on Learning.* New York, NY: Routledge.

Hawkey, E., and J. T. Nigg. 2014. "Omega-3 Fatty Acid and ADHD: Blood Level Analysis and Meta-analytic Extension of Supplementation Trials." *Clinical Psychology Review* 34(6): 496–505.

Hepark, S., L. Janssen, A. De Vries, P. L. Schoenberg, R. Donders, C. C. Kan, and A. E. Speckens. 2015. "The Efficacy of Adapted MBCT on Core Symptoms and Executive Functioning in Adults With ADHD: A Preliminary Randomized Controlled Trial." Nov 20. pii: 1087054715613587.

Holton, K. F., and J. T. Nigg. 2016. "The Association of Lifestyle Factors and ADHD in Children." *Journal of Attention Disorders* April 28. pii: 1087054716646452.

Hölzel, M., J. Carmody, M. Vangel, C. Congleton, S. M. Yerramsetti, T. Gard, and S. W. Lazar. 2011. "Mindfulness Practice Leads to Increases in Regional Brain Gray Matter Density." *Psychiatry Research* 191(1): 36–43.

Horvath, M., H. Herleman, and R. McKie. 2006. "Goal Orientation, Task Difficulty, and Task Interest: A Multilevel Analysis." *Motivation and Emotion* 30(2): 169–176.

Hvolby, A. 2015. "Associations of Sleep Disturbance with ADHD: Implications for Treatment." *ADHD Attention Deficit and Hyperactivity Disorders* 7(1): 1–18.

Insel, T. R., and L. J. Young. 2001. "The Neurobiology of Attachment." *Nature Reviews Neuroscience* 2(2): 129–136.

Jackson, J. N. S., and J. MacKillop. "Attention-Deficit/Hyperactivity Disorder and Monetary Delay Discounting: A Meta-analysis of Case-Control Studies." *Biological Psychiatry* 1(4): 316–325.

Jacobs, B., M., M. Schall, and A. B. Scheibel. 1993. "A Quantitative Dendritic Analysis of Wernicke's Area in Humans. II. Gender, Hemispheric, and Environmental Factors." *The Journal of Comparative Neurology* 327(1): 97–111.

Jacobson, T., and V. Hoffman. 1997. "Children's Attachment Representations: Longitudinal Relations to School Behavior and Academic Competency in Middle Childhood and Adolescence." *Developmental Psychology* 33(4): 703–10.

Jaffe, E. 2010. "This Side of Paradise: Discovering Why the Human Mind Needs Nature." *APS Observer* 23(5): 10–15.

James, W. 1890. *The Principles of Psychology*, Vol. 1. New York: Henry Holt, pp. 403–4.

Keltikangas-Järvinen, L., K. Räikkönen, J. Ekelund, and L. Peltonen. 2004. "Nature and Nurture in Novelty Seeking." *Molecular Psychiatry* 9(3): 308–311.

Khoury, B., T. Lecomte, G. Fortin, M. Masse, P. Therrien, V. Bouchard, et al. 2013. "Mindfulness-Based Therapy: A Comprehensive Meta-analysis." *Clinical Psychology Review* 33: 763–771.

Koemans, R. G., S. van Vroenhoven, A. Karreman, and M. H. Bekker. 2015. "Attachment and Autonomy Problems in Adults with ADHD." *Journal of Attention Disorders* 19(5): 435–46.

Kuyken, W., F. C. Warren, R. S. Taylor, B. Whalley, C. Crane, G. Bondolfi, et al. 2016. "Efficacy of Mindfulness-Based Cognitive Therapy in Prevention of Depressive Relapse: An Individual Patient Data Meta-analysis from Randomized

Trials." *JAMA Psychiatry*, April 27, 2016. doi: 10.1001/jama psychiatry. 2016.0076.

LaChance, L., K. McKenzie, V. H. Taylor, and S. N. Vigod. 2016. "Omega-6 to Omega-3 Fatty Acid Ratio in Patients with ADHD: A Meta-analysis." *Journal of the Canadian Academy of Child and Adolescent Psychiatry* 25(2): 87–96.

Larimer, M. E., R. S. Palmer, and G. A. Marlatt. 1999. "Relapse Prevention: An Overview of Marlatt's Cognitive-Behavioral Model." *Alcohol Research & Health* 23(2): 151–160.

Lazar, S. W., C. E. Kerr, R. H. Wasserman, J. R. Gray, D. N. Greve, M. T. Treadway, et al. 2005. "Meditation Experience Is Associated with Increased Cortical Thickness." *Neuroreport* 16(17): 1893–1897.

Lemcke, S., E. T. Parner, M. Bjerrum, P. H. Thomsen, and M. B. Lauritsen. 2016. "Early Development in Children Later Diagnosed with Disorders of Attention and Activity: A Longitudinal Study in the Danish National Birth Cohort." *European Child & Adolescent Psychiatry*, February 9.

Lenzi, D., C. Trentini, R. Tambelli, and P. Pantano. 2015. "Neural Basis of Attachment-Caregiving Systems Interaction: Insights from Neuroimaging Studies." *Frontiers in Psychology* 6: 1–7.

Linehan, M. 2003. *Walking Like Buffalo: Reflections on Mindfulness and DBT*. Behavioral Tech, LLC. Seattle, WA.

Linehan, M. M. 2014. *DBT Skills Training Manual, Second Edition*. New York, NY: Guilford Press.

Linton, S. J., K. Boersma, K. Vangronsveld, and A. Fruzzetti. 2012. "Painfully Reassuring? The Effects of Validation on Emotions and Adherence in a Pain Test." *European Journal of Pain* 16(4): 592–599.

Luders, E., N. Cherbuin, and C. Gaser 2016. "Estimating Brain Age Using High-Resolution Pattern Recognition: Younger Brains in Long-Term Meditation Practitioners." *Neuroimage* 134: 508–513. doi: 10.1016/j.neuroimage.2016.04.007.

Lutz, A., H. A. Slagter, J. D. Dunne, and R. J. Davidson. 2008. "Attention Regulation and Monitoring in Meditation." *Trends in Cognitive Sciences* 12(4): 163–169.

Maddock, R. J., G. A. Casazza, D. H. Fernandez, and M. I. Maddock. 2016. "Acute Modulation of Cortical Glutamate and GABA Content by Physical Activity." *The Journal of Neuroscience* 36(8): 2449–2457.

Martel, M., M. Nikolas, K. Jernigan, K. Friderici, I. Waldman, and J. Nigg. 2011. "The Dopamine Receptor D4 Gene (DRD4) Moderates Family Environmental Effects on ADHD." *Journal of Abnormal Child Psychology* 39(1): 1–10.

Mattfield, A. T., J. D. Gabrieli, J. Biederman, T. Spencer, A. Brown, A. Kotte, E. Kagan, and S. Whitfield-Gabrieli. 2014. "Brain Differences Between Persistent and Remitted Attention Deficit Hyperactivity Disorder." *Brain* 137(Pt 9): 2423–2428.

Matthews, M., J. T. Nigg, and D. A. Fair. 2014. "Attention Deficit Hyperactivity Disorder." *Current Topics in Behavioral Neurosciences* 16: 235–266.

Mayer, K., F. Blume, S. N. Wyckoff, L. L. Brokmeier, and U. Strehl. 2015. "Neurofeedback of Slow Cortical Potentials as a Treatment for Adults with Attention Deficit-/Hyperactivity Disorder." *Clinical Neurophysiology* 127(2): 1374–1386.

McCrae, R. R., and P. T. Costa Jr. 1987. "Validation of the Five-Factor Model of Personality Across Instruments and Observers." *Journal of Personality and Social Psychology* 52(1): 81–90.

McGonigal, K. 2013. *The Willpower Instinct: How Self-Control Works, Why It Matters, and What You Can Do to Get More of It.* New York, NY: Penguin Group.

McNab, F., A. Varrone, L. Farde, A. Jucaite, P. Bystritsky, H. Forssberg, and T. Klingberg. 2009. "Changes in Cortical Dopamine D1 Receptor Binding Associated with Cognitive Training." *Science* 323(5915): 800–802.

Medina, J. 2014. *Brain Rules: 12 Principles for Surviving and Thriving at Work, Home, and School.* Seattle, WA: Pear Press. (Also see http://www.brainrules.net.)

MedlinePlus. 2016. "Dietary Fats." Retrieved from http://www.nlm.nih.gov/medlineplus/dietaryfats.html.

Mehta, R., R. Zhu, and A. Cheema. 2012. "Is Noise Always Bad? Exploring the Effects of Ambient Noise on Creative Cognition." *Journal of Consumer Research* 39(4): 784–799.

Messamore, E., and R. K. McNamara. 2016. "Detection and Treatment of Omega-3 Fatty Acid Deficiency in Psychiatric Practice: Rationale and Implementation." *Lipids in Health and Disease* 15(1): 25.

Mickelson, K. D., R. C. Kessler, and P. R. Shaver. 1997. "Adult Attachment in a Nationally Representative Sample." *Journal of Personality and Social Psychology* 73(5): 1092–1106.

Mikulincer, M., O. Gillath, and P. R. Shaver. 2002. "Activation of the Attachment System in Adulthood: Threat-Related Primes Increase the Accessibility of Mental Representations of Attachment Figures." *Journal of Personality and Social Psychology* 83(4): 881–895.

Mikulincer, M., P. R. Shaver, O. Gillath, and R. A. Nitzberg. 2005. "Attachment, Caregiving, and Altruism: Boosting Attachment Security Increases Compassion and Helping." *Journal of Personality and Social Psychology* 89(5): 817–839.

Mitchell, J. T., L. Zylowska, and S. H. Kollins. 2015. "Mindfulness Meditation Training for Attention-Deficit/Hyperactivity Disorder in Adulthood: Current Empirical Support, Treatment Overview, and Future Directions." *Cognitive and Behavioral Practice* 22(2): 172–191.

Moffitt, T. E., R. Houts, P. Asherson, D. W. Belsky, D. L. Corcoran, M. Hammerle, et al. 2015. "Is Adult ADHD a Childhood-Onset Neurodevelopmental Disorder? Evidence from a

Four-Decade Longitudinal Cohort Study." *American Journal of Psychiatry* 172(10): 967–977.

Musser, E., S. Karalunas, N. Dieckmann, T. Peris, and J. T. Nigg. 2016. "Attention-Deficit/Hyperactivity Disorder Developmental Trajectories Related to Parental Expressed Emotion." *Journal of Abnormal Psychology* 125(2): 182–195.

Mutskov, V., A. Khalyfa, Y. Wang, A. Carreras, M. A. Nobrega, and D. Gozal. 2015. "Early-Life Physical Activity Reverses Metabolic and Foxo1 Epigenetic Misregulation Induced by Gestational Sleep Disturbance." *American Journal of Physiology—Regulatory, Integrative and Comparative Physiology* 308(5): R419–R430.

National Sleep Foundation. 2015. "How Much Sleep Do We Really Need?" Retrieved from http://sleepfoundation.org /how-sleep-works/how-much-sleep-do-we-really-need.

Neff, K. 2011. *Self-Compassion: The Proven Power of Being Kind to Yourself*. New York, NY: William Morrow.

Neff, K. D., Y. P. Hsieh, and K. Dejitterat. 2005. "Self-Compassion, Achievement Goals, and Coping with Academic Failure." *Self and Identity* 4(3): 263–287.

Neustadt, E. A., T. Chamorro-Premuzic, and A. Furnham. 2011. "Attachment at Work and Performance." *Attachment & Human Development* 13(5): 471–488.

Newman, K. M. 2015. "To Change Yourself, Change Your World." Retrieved from http://greatergood.berkeley.edu/article/item /to_change_yourself_change_your_world.

NICABM. 2016, February. *What Restores Aliveness and Vitality?* [Video file]. Retrieved from http://www.nicabm.com.

Nigg, J., S. Karalunas, and S. Mitchell. 2015. "Longitudinal Study of the Course of ADHD." Retrieved from http://www.ohsu .edu/xd/education/schools/school-of-medicine/departments /clinical-departments/psychiatry/research/adhd-attention-

disorders-study/current-research/longitudinal_study_adhd
.cfm.

Nigg, J. T., A. L. Elmore, N. Natarajan, K. H. Friderici, and M. A. Nikolas. 2015. "Variation in an Iron Metabolism Gene Moderates the Association Between Blood Lead Levels and Attention-Deficit/Hyperactivity Disorder in Children." *Psychological Science* 27(2): 257–269.

Nikitopoulos, J., K. Zohsel, D. Blomeyer, A. F. Buchmann, B. Schmid, C. Jennen-Steinmetz, et al. 2014. "Are Infants Differentially Sensitive to Parenting? Early Maternal Care, DRD4 Genotype and Externalizing Behavior During Adolescence." *Journal of Psychiatric Research* 59: 53–59.

Nowak, M. 2012. "Dealing with Difference: Diagnostic Labels, the Hunter-Farmer Metaphor, and Self-Referential Terms of Identity and Affiliation." Retrieved from http://education.jhu .edu/PD/newhorizons/Exceptional%20Learners/ADD%20 ADHD/Articles/Dealing%20with%20Difference/.

NPR. 2011. *Help! Radiolab*, season 9, episode 3. Retrieved from http://www.radiolab.org/story/117165-help.

Oaten, M., and K. Cheng. 2006. "Longitudinal Gains in Self-Regulation from Regular Physical Exercise." *British Journal of Health Psychology* 11(4): 717–733.

Pallini, S. and F. Laghi. 2012. "Attention and Attachment Related Behavior Toward Professional Caregivers in Child Care Centers: A New Measure for Toddlers." *The Journal of Genetic Psychology* 173(2):158–74.

Pearson, J. L., D. A. Cohn, P. A. Cowan, and C. P. Cowan. 1994. "Earned- and Continuous-Security in Adult Attachment: Relation to Depressive Symptomatology and Parenting Style." *Development and Psychopathology* 6(2): 359–373.

Pelham, W. E., D. A. Waschbusch, B. Hoza, E. M. Gnagy, A. R. Greiner, S. E. Sams, G. Vallano, A. Majumdar, and R. E. Carter. 2011. "Music and Video Movies as Distractors for

Boys with ADHD in the Classroom: Comparison with Controls, Individual Differences, and Medication Effects." *Journal of Abnormal Child Psychology* 39: 1085–1098. doi:10.1007/s10802–011–9529-z.

Pennsylvania State University. 2006. "Hydrogenated Vegetable Oils and Trans Fatty Acids." Prepared by J. Lynne Brown, associate professor of food science. Retrieved from http://extension.psu.edu/publications/uk093.

Pietromonaco, P. R., and S. I. Powers. 2015. "Attachment and Health-Related Physiological Stress Processes." *Current Opinion in Psychology* 1: 34–39.

Pontifex, M. B., B. J. Saliba, L. B. Raine, D. L. Picchietti, and C. H. Hillman. 2013. "Exercise Improves Behavioral, Neurocognitive, and Scholastic Performance in Children with Attention-Deficit/Hyperactivity Disorder." *The Journal of Pediatrics* 162(3): 543–51.

Rangarajo, S., D. F. Levey, K. Nho, N. Jain, K. D. Andrews, H. Le-Niculescu, D. R. Salomon, A. J. Saykin, M. Petrascheck, and A. B. Niculescu. 2016. "Mood, Stress and Longevity: Convergence on ANK3." *Molecular Psychiatry*, May 24. doi: 10.1038/mp.2016.65.

Reinberg, S. 2009. "Motivation May Be at Root of ADHD: Scans Suggest That Symptoms Stem from Deficits in Brain's Rewards System." *HealthDay*, September 8, 2009. Retrieved from https://consumer.healthday.com/kids-health-information-23/attention-deficit-disorder-adhd-news-50/motivation-may-be-at-root-of-adhd-630780.html.

Richards, D. A., and A. C. Schat. 2011. "Attachment at (Not to) Work: Applying Attachment Theory to Explain Individual Behavior in Organizations." *Journal of Applied Psychology* 96(1): 169–182.

Rodriguez-Leyva, D., and G. W. Pierce. 2010. "The Cardiac and Haemostatic Effects of Dietary Hempseed." *Nutrition & Metabolism* 7(32).

Saunders, R., D. Jacobvitz, M. Zaccagnino, L. M. Beverung, and N. Hazen. 2011. "Pathways to Earned-Security: The Role of Alternative Support Figures." *Attachment & Human Development* 13(4): 403–420.

Schore, A. N. 2001. "Effects of a Secure Attachment Relationship on Right Brain Development, Affect Regulation, and Infant Mental Health." *Infant Mental Health Journal* 22(1–2): 7–66.

Shenk, C. E., and A. E. Fruzzetti. 2011. "The Impact of Validating and Invalidating Responses on Emotional Reactivity." *Journal of Social and Clinical Psychology* 30(2): 163–183.

Siegel, D. 1999. *The Developing Mind: How Relationships and the Brain Interact to Shape Who We Are.* New York, NY: The Guilford Press.

Siegel, D. 2010. Mindsight: *The New Science of Personal Transformation.* New York, NY: Random House.

Siegel, D. 2012a. *The Developing Mind: How Relationships and the Brain Interact to Shape Who We Are* (2nd edition). New York, NY: The Guilford Press.

Siegel, D. 2012b. *Pocket Guide to Interpersonal Neurobiology: An Integrative Handbook of the Mind.* New York, NY: W. W. Norton & Company.

Simmons, D. 2008. Epigenetic influence and disease. *Nature Education* 1(1): 6.

Soler, R. E., K. D. Leeks, L. R. Buchanan, R. C. Brownson, G. W. Heath, D. H. Hopkins, and Task Force on Community Preventive Services. 2010. "Point-of-Decision Prompts to Increase Stair Use: A Systematic Review Update." *American Journal of Preventive Medicine* 38(2 Suppl): S292–S300.

Sroufe, A., and D. Siegel. n.d. *The Verdict Is In: The Case for Attachment Theory.* Retrieved from http://www.drdansiegel.com/uploads/1271-the-verdict-is-in.pdf.

Storebø, O. J., P. D. Rasmussen, and E. Simonsen. 2016. "Association Between Insecure Attachment and ADHD: Environmental Mediating Factors." *Journal of Attention Disorders* 20(2): 187–196.

Suttie, J. 2015. "Stopping the Distraction Epidemic." Retrieved from http://greatergood.berkeley.edu/article/item/stopping_the_distraction_epidemic.

Thakkar, V. G. 2013. "Diagnosing the Wrong Deficit." *New York Times*, Sunday Review, Opinion, April 27, 2013. Retrieved from http://www.nytimes.com/2013/04/28/opinion/sunday/diagnosing-the-wrong-deficit.html?_r=0.

Torgersen, T., B. Gjervan, M. B. Lensing, and K. Rasmussen. 2016. "Optimal Management of ADHD in Older Adults." *Neuropsychiatric Disease and Treatment* 12: 79–87.

Tsubota, K. 2015. "Aging Science Comes of Age." *npj Aging and Mechanisms of Disease* 1: 15007.

Turner, C. 2015. "The Teacher Who Believes Math Equals Love." Retrieved from http://www.npr.org/sections/ed/2015/03/09/376596585/the-teacher-who-believes-math-equals-love.

UCLA Mindful Awareness Research Center. n.d. Resources. Retrieved from http://marc.ucla.edu/body.cfm?id=38.

Van den Bos, R., and D. de Ridder. 2006. "Evolved to Satisfy Our Immediate Needs: Self-Control and the Rewarding Properties of Food." *Appetite* 47(1): 24–59.

Van Dongen, H. P. A., G. Maislin, J. M. Mullington, and D. F. Dinges. 2003. "The Cumulative Cost of Additional Wakefulness: Dose-Response Effects on Neurobehavioral Functions and Sleep Physiology from Chronic Sleep Restriction and Total Sleep Deprivation." *Sleep* 26(2): 117–126.

Verbeke, W., R. P. Bagozzi, and W. E. van den Berg. 2014. "The Role of Attachment Styles in Regulating the Effects of Dopamine on the Behavior of Salespersons." *Frontiers in Human Neuroscience* 8: 32.

Volkow, N. D., G. J. Wang, S. H. Kollins, T. L. Wigal, J. H. Newcorn, F. Telang, et al. 2009. "Evaluating Dopamine Reward Pathway in ADHD." *Journal of the American Medical Association* 302(10): 1084–1091.

Volkow, N. D., G. J. Wang, J. H. Newcorn, S. H. Kollins, T. L. Wigal, F. Telang, et al. 2011. "Motivation Deficit in ADHD Is Associated with Dysfunction of the Dopamine Reward Pathway." *Molecular Psychiatry* 16(11): 1147–54.

Vrtička, P., and P. Vuilleumier. 2012. "Neuroscience of Human Social Interactions and Adult Attachment Style." *Frontiers in human neuroscience*, 6:212. doi: 10.3389/fnhum.2012.00212.

Walsh, C. n.d. "Urge Surfing." Retrieved from http://www.mindfulness.org.au/#!urge-surfing/h57he on May 28, 2016.

Wansink, B. 1996. "Can Package Size Accelerate Usage Volume?" *Journal of Marketing* 60(3): 1–14.

Wansink, B., and K. van Ittersum. 2005. "Shape of Glass and Amount of Alcohol Poured: Comparative Study of Effect of Practice and Concentration." *BMJ* 331(7531): 1512–1514.

Waters, C. 2014. "Fast Lane: Forget Gamification It's All About Playification." *SmartCompany*, October 6, 2014. Retrieved from http://www.smartcompany.com.au/growth/44054-fast-lane-forget-gamification-it-s-all-about-playification.

*Web*MD. 2015. "The Facts on Omega-3 Fatty Acids." Retrieved from http://www.webmd.com/healthy-aging/omega-3-fatty-acids-fact-sheet.

White, H. A., and P. Shah. 2006. "Uninhibited Imaginations: Creativity in Adults with Attention-Deficit/Hyperactivity Disorder." *Personality and Individual Differences* 40(6): 1121–1131.

White, H. A., and P. Shah. 2011. "Creative Style and Achievement in Adults with Attention-Deficit/Hyperactivity Disorder." *Personality and Individual Differences* 50(5): 673–677.

Wiggins, G. A., and J. Bhattacharya. 2014. "Mind the Gap: An Attempt to Bridge Computational and Neuroscientific Approaches to Study Creativity." *Frontiers in Human Neuroscience* 8: 540.

Williams, J. G., S. K. Stark, and E. E. Foster. 2008. "Start Today or the Very Last Day? The Relationships Among Self-Compassion, Motivation, and Procrastination." *American Journal of Psychological Research* 4(1): 37–44.

Wohl, M. J. A., T. A. Pychyl, and S. H. Bennett. 2010. "I Forgive Myself, Now I Can Study: How Self-Forgiveness for Procrastinating Can Reduce Future Procrastination." *Personality and Individual Differences* 48(7): 803–808.

Zabelina, D. L., D. Condon, and M. Beeman. 2014. "Do Dimensional Psychopathology Measures Relate to Creative Achievement or Divergent Thinking?" *Frontiers in Psychology* 5 (1029). doi:10.3389/fpsyg.2014.01029.

Zak, P. J. 2013. "How Stories Change the Brain." Retrieved from http://greatergood.berkeley.edu/article/item/how_stories _change_brain.

Zheng, Y., B. T. Joyce, E. Colicino, L. Liu, W. Zhang, Q. Dai, et al. 2016. "Blood Epigenetic Age May Predict Cancer Incidence and Mortality." *EBioMedicine*. doi: 10.1016/jebiom.2016.02.008.

Zylowska, L. 2012. *The Mindfulness Prescription for Adult ADHD: An 8-Step Program for Strengthening Attention, Managing Emotions, and Achieving Your Goals.* Boston, MA: Trumpeter Books.

Zylowska L., D. L. Ackerman, M. H. Yang, J. L. Futrell, N. L. Horton, T. S. Hale, C. Pataki, and S. L. Smalley. 2008. "Mindfulness Meditation Training in Adults and Adolescents with ADHD: A Feasibility Study." *Journal of Attention Disorders* 11(6): 737–46.

Greg Crosby, MA, LPC, is a practicing therapist and college and graduate school instructor. In 1994, he started the first adult attention deficit/hyperactivity disorder (ADHD) group for the Kaiser Permanente Northwest Region, and has been working with the Oregon Attorney Assistance Program providing ADHD workshops since 2013. Crosby is a certified group psychotherapist and group psychotherapy fellow. He teaches adult ADHD classes at Portland State University and Marylhurst University. Crosby offers workshops on ADHD for professionals, and has a private practice where he works with adults diagnosed with ADHD.

Tonya K. Lippert, PhD, works for Kaiser Permanente's mental health and social work departments, where, among other duties, she leads adult attention deficit/hyperactivity disorder (ADHD) groups. Lippert has written several research articles, as well as children's books during her free time. She also knows what it's like to live with ADHD up close thanks to her spouse and one of her children (both of whom generously shared experiences and contributed ideas for the book).

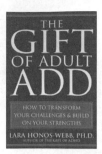

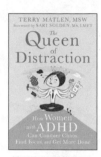
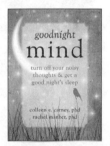

Register your **new harbinger** titles for additional benefits!

When you register your **new harbinger** title—purchased in any format, from any source—you get access to benefits like the following:

- Downloadable accessories like printable worksheets and extra content

- Instructional videos and audio files

- Information about updates, corrections, and new editions

Not every title has accessories, but we're adding new material all the time.

Access free accessories in 3 easy steps:

1. Sign in at NewHarbinger.com (or **register** to create an account).

2. Click on **register a book**. Search for your title and click the **register** button when it appears.

3. Click on the **book cover or title** to go to its details page. Click on **accessories** to view and access files.

That's all there is to it!

If you need help, visit:

NewHarbinger.com/accessories

new harbinger
CELEBRATING
40 YEARS